Winning SEASONS

DISCOVERING THE *Champion* WITHIN

JOE CROCHET

outskirts press

TABLE OF CONTENTS

THE CITADEL FOOTBALL TEAM 2015

FRONT ROW: Mark Thomas, Vinny Miller, Mariel Cooper, Nick Willis, James Riley, Mike Mabry, Sam Frye, Mitchell Jeter, Greg Dicocco, Charles Clark, Alex Glover, Brandon Eakins, Austin Jordan

SECOND ROW: Shy Phillips, Deandre Schoultz, Jorian Jordan, Dee Delaney, Joe Crochet, Dane Anderson, Rod Johnson, Israel Battle, Khafari Buffalo, Jordan Black, Ben Roberts, Shon Belton

THIRD ROW: Jalen Lampkin, Curt Nixon, Josh Massey, Cam Jackson, Dom Allen, AJ Vandiver, Malik Diggs, Dondray Copeland, Tyus Carter, Aron Spann, III, Reggie Williams, Jonathan Dorogy, Jordan Williams

FOURTH ROW: Craig Miller, Tyler Jackson, Jauveer Hammond, Za'von Whitaker, Phil Davis, Quinlan Washington, Evan Mcfield, Tyler Renew, Lorenzo Ward, J.J Baldwin, Isaiah Smith, Kailik Williams

FIFTH ROW: Seth Greer, Trey Nelson, Tevin Floyd, Jordan Thomas, Grant Drakeford, Donald Rutledge, Curt Nixon, Carl Cunningham, Caleb Bennett, Kevin Graham, Nathan Peeples, Myles Pierce, Ryan Bednar, Tyler Davis

THE CITADEL FOOTBALL TEAM 2015

SIXTH ROW: Greg Pappas, Russell Hubbs, Lovequan Scott, Kyle Weaver, Austin Harrell, Lee Riley, Hunter Morris, Emmet Howle, Hugh Mcfaddin, Patrick Keefe, Zack Vanalstine, Ken Allen

SEVENTH ROW: Mike Rentz, Nick Jeffreys, Bradley Carter, Isaiah Pinson, Sydney Martin, Drew Campbell, Andrew Laulusa, Tristan Harkleroad, Caleb Hester, Rudder Brown, Cameron Scott

EIGHTH ROW: Jake Riggs, Whit Miller, Will Vanvick, Tre'von White, Adam Wawrzynski, Attorney Gallman, Noah Dawkins, Jalon Williams, Jonathan King, Eric Goins

NINETH ROW: Floris Mendonca, RaShan Frost, Joel Taylor, Ron Boyd, Tripp Weaver, Roy Tesh, Jimmy Long, Brian Rucker, Brent Thompson, Mike Houston, Maurice Drayton, Blake Harrell, J.P. Gunter, John Ward, Donnell Boucher, Stephen Reich, Mike Morgan, Paul Standard, DaSean Daniels, Price Blagg

FOREWORD

The Citadel, in my mind, is an elite institution that has a pristine respect for itself. It's as highly regarded by the people who are currently there as it is by the alumni who come out of it—alumni who have experienced successes in life, in the military, and in politics. I think that they have had a significant influence on the Southeast.

I always think back to the first week I was on campus after I had taken the job. It was Saturday morning, 6 a.m., and I was walking into the main lobby of Seignious Hall. As I was on my way to the coaches' office, I tripped over a kid sleeping on the floor. I looked up, and there were like forty kids in sleeping bags everywhere upstairs. *What in the world is this?* I thought. I had no clue what was happening. That was the beginning of my education in what the knobs go through.

I think the culture was good there. Coach Higgins did a great job recruiting young men, and I thought the football program was in good order. Yet there was something lacking. What was lacking was a set end-goal, a winning mindset. Nobody was walking around claiming that we were going to win a conference championship. As I began talking with some of the more prestigious alumni, I kept hearing the same thing over and over again: *We understand that it's challenging to coach at The Citadel, and it's challenging to compete athletically on the field because of all the other things that you have to deal with. We understand that you are not going to win all the time, but the main thing is we just want our teams to play well and to represent the institution with class.* Everybody said the same thing. These are not winning proclamations. That was the first glaring problem I saw.

Back then, I felt like the only way we could win a championship was to use our offense and to become the most physical team in the league. That was our edge, and we would play with great discipline, great intensity, and extreme physicality. After that first year, I felt like we had built something that could compete and win championships. In my opinion, most college football teams are not physical or disciplined. Our goal was to win a Southern Conference Championship. If we wanted to compete—if there was going to be a championship and they were going to give out a trophy—then that is what we were competing for, just like everyone else.

When I started talking about this, I had people telling me to be careful. Don't start talking championships, they said. They warned that if I built it up too much and then things didn't go well, I could lose the morale of the team.

I refused to accept that. You play to win, I countered. I felt that this was the biggest hurdle we had to overcome. Another hurdle was getting all the players on the same page and getting them to believe in each other, getting them to trust each other, getting them to trust the coaching staff, and getting them to trust that everybody was on the same page, working toward one common goal. That was the culture we were trying to create and were able to carry on with Coach Thompson as I left.

In order to establish a championship program, I knew that the first thing I had to do was unify the locker room, to instill a sense of family and a sense of trust in the players. This was my guiding principle. Each team member had to do his job and trust that the brother lining up next to him was going to do his. We are all accountable to each other. As a defensive lineman playing five-technique, most of the time you (Joe) had a job to cover the C-gap in the run game. You couldn't be jumping to the B-gap, trying to make a play that belongs to the three-technique. You had to do your job and trust that the three-technique, Mitchel, was going to do his job. When we started, that was not even close to being there—the team needed discipline. We tried really hard to create that trust in one another and then hammer home that we were all in this thing together. We were all accountable to one other. We had to give tremendous effort to execute at a high level, and to do everything we were required to do. We either win together or lose together. At the end of the day, we all needed one another.

Instilling an incredible work ethic is the other requirement for creating a championship program. There is zero tolerance for anything less than your best effort. I really try to beat on this. I will not tolerate a guy that is lazy, nor will I tolerate a guy I cannot trust. At the beginning, we had to get rid of a couple of players because they could not be trusted. They were not all in. They were not committed to practicing tough, playing tough, and playing with that fire and intensity. The sport is meant to be played with a lot of intensity, a lot of fire, and a lot of passion. That type of play is contagious. You know when a guy makes a great play, everybody starts celebrating and it rubs off on others and soon everyone is playing with more fire and at a higher intensity.

We were always going to represent the program in a first-class manner: off the field, in the classroom, and around the community. Our last name was The Citadel. My motto is: *As long as you are where you are supposed to be, doing what you are supposed to be doing with the people you are supposed to be doing it with you will never get into trouble.* I remember coming to JMU and telling them that the team I just left in Charleston would beat them by thirty. Granted, there is no comparison in talents; but they had none of the traits and characteristics that you guys had.

Going into 2015, I knew we were getting closer, and the big thing was that we had to have a good start. I did not factor in just how quickly we had turned the players and the coaching staff's culture around. Most of the time, that doesn't happen until all the older players graduate. But the thing is that you guys (the class of 2016) bought in and had a tremendous work ethic. The 2015 season was a year earlier than what I had expected. That season will always be a special season to me.

My favorite memory of that 2015 season was beating the University of South Carolina. William Brice Stadium was the perfect storm. We were standing there in pre-game warmups and they (the Gamecocks) had zero intensity. There was no fire or motivation. We didn't think Orth, the quarterback, could beat us throwing the ball, and we were playing stack-the-box to shut down the run. They didn't appear to be a physical bunch and we knew we could really do some damage with our base offense. Our plan was to shut down the run and make them have to place the ball with their kicking game and just manage the field position. With Spurrier resigning in the middle of the season and the Gamecocks just coming off a close loss to Florida, we were going into a perfect storm. I looked at Coach Thompson and said, "If we have a couple of things come our way early… we are going to beat them."

We wanted to see how they guarded the perimeter with the first play. We saw something, and the next play Cam Jackson took it to the house and that was the spark we needed. From there on, it was a dog fight. My thing was that I didn't want our guys to lose their heads with the atmosphere of 77,500 people. I didn't want them to lose their composure. My mindset was to stay positive and stay focused on the next play. To not get caught up in the moment. We were prepared for this moment. When James tackled the running back to win the game, it was a complete euphoria; we were overwhelmed with emotion because we had worked so hard and the game the week before against Chattanooga had been such a painful loss. It was almost vindication.

Post-Game USC vs The Citadel Interview

I was really ticked off by the comments Paul Finebaum made about us with the Florida State game the year before. I thought it was extremely disrespectful and showed no class. He was the sideline guy for that game, and most of the time as the head coach you talk to those guys during that week of prep, especially on game day. It was obvious that he didn't do his homework, nor did he do anything for The Citadel. He didn't talk to me at any point of time. He didn't think it was going to be a game. It was just a complete and utter lack of respect. Fast-forward to the USC game, where the game was tight and we were going back and forth with lead changes; the next thing you know, he was on our sideline. Then suddenly it was a game and he had to do something for the TV telecast for The Citadel. So, everybody knew he was on our sideline the second half, and we stopped them on fourth down and were getting ready for the victory kneel. One of the coaches came up to me and said, "Don't you let up on Finebaum when it comes to the post-game interview. You make sure he recognizes that he disrespected us, our entire school, our program, and he needs to make sure that he knows what he did." There was a message in the words that I was saying in the interview that were firmly at him. He should have more respect for our players, our program, and the young men we have. We are capable of so many things because of our intangibles.

FCS vs. FBS Bias

The biggest difference between FCS and FBS is resources. FBS has twenty-two more scholarships, but then you have to factor in cost of attendance, support staff, and all the things the upper-tier Power Five schools have. It's a night and day difference as far as the funding that goes into them. Now when you start talking twenty-two more scholarships, that's an entire starting offense and starting defense of players. Those games, in my opinion, should never be competitive, but they often are because more and more FCS teams are knocking off FBS teams. I think it has to do with a lack of respect from the FBS opponents. We had players at The Citadel that could play at the FBS level, but they were never given a chance to do so, and that is what made us so dangerous. When you put it into a sixty-minute game, anything can happen. You see it more and more… FCS teams knocking off Power Five teams. I think there should be more respect for the FCS division, because there are quality players and quality coaches at this level. The perception is "Oh, they're FCS," but in reality, if you break it down, many of the coaches I've worked with have NFL and Power Five FBS experience, as well as former FCS Division II players that I coached who went on to play in the NFL or in Canada.

Though the fans might never truly change their viewpoint, those coaches at the Power Five level understand. Jimbo Fisher, former head coach of Florida State, said, "I understand exactly what your level is. I used to be an FCS coach. I used to be a Division II Coach." They understand that there are quality programs, players, and coaches at the FCS level. I do not think there that it will ever change from the Power Five in FBS. The arrogance of those fans will always look down on lower-tier programs. I think that FBS and major FCS teams in the next five to ten years are going to see a major change there, as far as revenues, funding, and other resources that will close that gap.

Your will to prepare has to be greater than your will to win. That is the philosophy that I developed as a high school coach. When it's game day and you get out on that field, everybody wants to win, everybody wants to beat their chest and be the victor and be in the spotlight; however, the ones that truly achieve success at a high level are the ones who are just as motivated in January and February when there are no spotlights or TV cameras on them. They understand that you have to train at a high level on a daily basis—not just on the Thursday before a game. That's what gives them the ability to dominate. To me, that's the difference factor between winning or losing.

I will be forever grateful for the opportunity I had at The Citadel, because the experience taught me more about running a football program than any other program could ever have done—all the things I had to handle on a daily basis. To be able to take the program from where it was to where we got it was historic. This had only been done once before.

Winning a Southern Conference Championship, beating South Carolina, the walk-off kick by Eric Goins in the playoffs against Coastal Carolina—all these things were historic, and I will forever have pride of accomplishment regarding what we were able to achieve together.

The Citadel is a very special place that is steeped in tradition, and it was great to be a part of a football program that represented the institution the way we did. That is forever going to be one of the highlights in my coaching career. Those memories are some of the greatest memories of my life. I appreciate everything that my players, the coaches, and The Citadel family were able to give.

Mike Houston
Head Coach of James Madison University,
Former Head Coach at The Citadel 2014 - 2015

*"All the efforts of a successful person
lie beneath the surface."*

-STEVE MUELLER

THANK YOU!

All things are possible because of God, and it is through His grace that I have been able to accomplish many great things; However, I did not do it alone. *My Winning Seasons* is dedicated to the 2015 Citadel Football team coaches and players, all our friends, family, alumni, and supporters who have given so much to our program. Without them, none of this would be possible.

I would like to give a special thank you to Mrs. Marjorie Maxon and Mrs. Helen Vanvick for their great photographs documenting the two best football seasons in the history of this great institution. Thank you, Floris and his video staff, for documenting these two great seasons. Thank you, Ms. Kate Brown, J.B. Weber, Kirsten Schumy and the entire Academic Support Center, because without them my academic endeavor of graduating early would have never come to fruition, nor would have many of the cadets and cadet athletes been able to accomplish everything they desired to accomplish academically. Thank you to Andy Clawson and The Sports Medicine Staff for the many years of dedicated service to this great institution and keeping our athletes and cadets healthy.

Thank you, General Rosa, for all your support and everything you have done for our program and for this great institution. Thank you,

Captain Paluso, for helping bridge the gap between student athletes and the Corps and helping shift the culture at The Citadel. Thank you, Lieutenant Colonel Panton, for your guidance as Lima's Company TAC throughout my tenure and helping my classmates and me to thrive throughout our military and academic duties as cadets.

I would like to thank The Citadel, The Citadel Football Association, The Brigadier Foundation, and The Citadel Alumni Association for making all this possible. Lastly, thank you, Charlie Baker, for allowing me to be on your scholarship and thank you to everyone who helped me get here.

I want to send a special thank you to all of my friends and family back home. Without your support, none of this would have been possible. Lastly, thank you to The Tucker Football League, St. Thomas More and St. Pius X family for helping me find my path.

IN LOVING MEMORY OF
MITCHELL JETER

The one thing about Mitchell Jeter I think all of us will never forget was that when he walked into a room, whether it was a bad day or a good day, he always had that big smile and filled the room with his presence. I loved his personality, I loved the person he was, and that is one thing that will always stick out to me. His senior year was a dominant performance by himself, and really, that came from his buying into everything we talked about. I will forever remember him as one of the great stories of transformation from the time he got there to the time he left. It certainly is a tragedy that he is no longer with us, but I will never forget him.

-Mike Houston, Former Head Football Coach
at The Citadel (2014- 2015)

IN LOVING MEMORY, OF
MIKE GROSHON, CLASS OF 1976

"It is not how much you do,
but how much love you put in the doing."

-Mother Teresa,
Catholic patron saint of missionaries

> *"It's not the size of the dog in the fight, it's the size of the fight in the dog."*
>
> – MARK TWAIN

C

INTRODUCTION

I was born on April 8, 1994, at Dekalb General Hospital just outside Decatur, Georgia. My parents—Eileen, a banker, and Donald, a physical therapist—are also from the area. My brother Daniel, federal consultant, was a former middle linebacker for Cornell's Big Red football team.

Growing up, I always loved playing sports. I started playing soccer in kindergarten. By the second grade I signed up for my first football and baseball seasons at Tucker Fitzgerald Field. I picked up basketball in the fourth grade and continued to play football for The Tucker Lions, the number one Pop Warner program in the Southeast. My academic career started off at St. Thomas More Elementary and Middle School in Decatur, Georgia. This is where I first started my relationship with God. My parents were married in St. Thomas More's church. I was baptized there and, along with many of my relatives, received all of my sacraments there. If you can't tell… I was born and raised by a Catholic family; however, like everyone in their religious quest, I have had my doubts and questions like many other people do. In this narrative I will unveil my journey with life, religion, and my ultimate pursuit of happiness, which to me means winning in life and in football. I went to high school at St. Pius X Catholic High School. I lettered in three sports (basketball, baseball, and football) and received the GHSA All-State Linebacker accolade my senior year. I signed a full four-and-a-half-year football scholarship to play football at The Citadel, The Military College of South Carolina, where I earned both a bachelor's of science in business administration and a master's in business administration.

One of the greatest lessons I gained from my education is the importance of continuing to learn. As long as I'm learning, I'm developing into a better person.

My Winning Seasons documents my experience from 2012-2016 as a student-athlete at The Citadel. It's the true story of a young kid from Stone Mountain, Georgia who took a chance by selecting the road less traveled and came out a man at the other side.

The Citadel, founded in 1842, has a long tradition of discipline and is known for instilling in its cadets the pillars of honor, duty, and respect. Many of our nation's heroes, men and women who have made the ultimate sacrifice for our freedom, started their journey at this great institution. For many, the journey through The Citadel is known as the road less traveled. A select few have earned the privilege of walking across the stage in McAlister Field House to receive a diploma. The South Carolina Corps of Cadets has a special place in my heart because it has made me into the man I am today. I do not know where I would be today if I had not decided to enroll at The Citadel or to play football in college.

Football was first played at The Citadel in 1907. The current stadium, Johnson Hagood Memorial Stadium (named after Brigadier General Johnson Hagood), was purchased by The Citadel from the

City of Charleston in 1963. The history of the stadium itself is deserving of its own book. One day I will write that book. It will tell the story of football greats such as Stump Mitchell, John Small, Nehemiah Broughton, and many others. It will recount notorious games such as the 1983 and 1984 FCS Championships and the Division I-A and Division I-AA Medal of Honor Bowls in 2014 and 2015.

The City of Charleston is consistently lauded as one of the best cities in the world in which to live, ranked #1 by *Forbes*, *Travel & Leisure*, *Business Insider* and Charleston's very own *Post and Courier*. The people there are magnificent, the food is delectable, and the history is rich. I urge each of my readers to visit Charleston at least once in their lifetime. Go to the places I talk about in this book such as the Battery, Rainbow Row, the city market on Market Street, the bars on King Street and Calhoun Street, Sullivan's Island lighthouse, Isle of Palms, Folly Beach, Dewees Island, Mount Pleasant, and, of course, The Citadel. The City of Charleston will not disappoint.

THE DASH

I read of a man who stood to speak at the funeral of a friend.
He referred to the dates on the tombstone from the beginning…to the end.
He noted that first came the date of birth and spoke of the following date with tears,
but he said what mattered most of all was the dash between those years.

For that dash represents all the time that they spent alive on earth.
And now only those who loved them know what that little line is worth.
For it matters not, how much we own, the cars…the house…the cash.
What matters is how we live and love and how we spend our dash.

So, think about this long and hard. Are there things you'd like to change?
For you never know how much time is left that can still be rearranged.
If we could just slow down enough to consider what's true and real
and always try to understand the way other people feel.

And be less quick to anger and show appreciation more
and love the people in our lives like we've never loved before.
If we treat each other with respect and more often wear a smile,
remembering that this special dash might only last a little while.

So, when your eulogy is being read, with your life's actions to rehash…
would you be proud of the things they say about how you spent your dash?

Linda Ellis

"The journey of a thousand miles begins with one step."

-LAO TZU

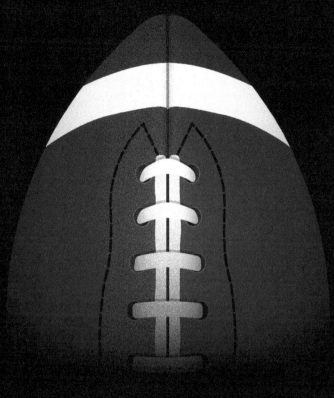

YEAR ONE

Red-Shirt Season

Chapter 1:

MATRICULATION DAY

It was the last day of February 2017, and I was sitting on a plane, making my way back to Atlanta from Minneapolis where I had been visiting my girlfriend Emily. I looked out the window at the workers loading suitcases onto the plane, marveling at how they could move under the encumbrance of winter coats, scarves and gloves. (If you want to visit the Twin Cities, I recommend going during the summer months. February is a little chilly, to say the least.)

"Excuse me, sir," said the young girl seated next to me.

"Yes ma'am, how might I help you?"

"Well, I can't help but admire that gold ring on your right hand. What does it stand for? Is it a championship ring?"

I smiled and told her it was actually a class ring from The Citadel. Her eyes widened.

"You went to The Citadel?" her mother chimed in. "I've heard so many great things about that institution. Did you go through a plebe year?"

I told her I did and that we called it the knob year because freshman cadets had to shave their heads bald to resemble the butt end of a door knob and keep it that way for an entire ten months while going through the process of being broken down, only to be built back up.

She asked to see pictures, but I didn't have any on my phone. "I might be able to show you some once we land," I said.

"Oh, that would be lovely!" said the mother. I smiled at her and turned the other way.

Twenty minutes later, we were well on our way and I was dozing off with my head against the window.

"Excuse me, sir. Can I get you something to drink?" This time it was the flight attendant. I ordered a water and considered how important water is to human life. I had read somewhere that the average human body is sixty percent water and remembered how essential it was to always have a jug of water with me back at The Citadel, back during my glory days. (Charleston's heat and humidity are no joke—they could dehydrate a river if given the chance.) I always carried a gallon jug of water around and made sure to finish that gallon of water by nightfall. I leaned back in my seat, letting out a loud yawn, remembering my glory days, looking off into the distance at the sea of clouds beneath the plane, wondering what everyone else from The Citadel was up to.

"Excuse me, mister?" the little girl said to me, waking me from my half-sleep. "Can you tell me about your experience at The Citadel? My dad talks about it all the time, and I just wish that he was here to meet you."

"Where is your dad? I would love to meet him too," I say, curious about why this young girl's father would be talking about the college. What was his connection to it?

"He's stationed in Iraq and won't be home for another month." A look of sadness flashed through her eyes.

"Young lady, I would be more than happy to tell you about my experience at The Citadel. What's your name?" I asked.

"Mary."

"Very pleased to meet you," I said, extending my hand for a shake. "I'm Joe Crochet. Where do I begin? How about with the first day?" She nodded in agreement, her eyes now filled with wonder. "Of course, I remember it like it was yesterday. Trey, quarterback at St. Pius X Catholic High School; Ty, running back from Dunwoody High; Kyle, offensive lineman from Hilton Head Christian Academy; Caleb, linebacker from Blue Ridge High; Eric, punter and kicker from Oakton High; Preston, linebacker from Chapman High. We were all waiting in line to matriculate, which means like officially enter, or kick off the first year. It's something you have to do on the first day."

That day was the beginning of my first long stint away from home, and I was lucky that I didn't have to jump into the boat alone. Trey was my close friend from St. Pius X High School, where we'd both played on the football and basketball teams. Similarly, Ty and I had played football together for the Tucker Lions in the fifth grade (and had won a championship, I must add). He and I had lost touch when he transferred to Peachtree Middle School, then reconnected years later when Dunwoody played St. Pius X for the region championship.

I knew some of the other guys too, because as football players we'd been required to show up earlier in the summer for training. Having spent that time with Kyle, Caleb, and Eric, I knew we would become great friends. At six foot two, two hundred and seventy pounds, Kyle looked like an All-American defensive tackle. Caleb, who weighed at least two hundred and twenty-five pounds, looked like he had worked out every minute of his life. Eric looked like he could play outside linebacker or safety for an SEC school.

I remember feeling nervous and excited. And tired—I had not slept the night before. Matriculation day is the first day of initiation into The Citadel. It's a proud moment for parents and siblings to watch as a loved one drives through Lesesne Gates to embark on his or her four-year journey. To the parents, this day at The Citadel is the first day of a historic event known as Challenge Week, but to all cadets and to Citadel men and women, the first seven days are collectively known as "Hell Week."

"Hell, as in where the devil lives?" my young listener interjected.

"Yes. Hell, as in the place where no one ever wants to go, the place where all evil resides. At The Citadel, Hell Week is the initiation week when a knob learns to endure being broken down, having his human rights stripped away. A knob has about as much rights as a doormat."

"That's silly! Doormats don't have rights."

"Exactly my point, Mary."

At the time, dear reader, we did not quite know what we were letting ourselves in for. I remember joking around with my teammates, thinking the upperclassmen were merely trying to scare us with their stories of what was to come. It couldn't possibly be as bad as they made it out to be, could it? Well, let me tell you—they were not kidding. Reality was about to hit us hard in the face.

So anyway, back to the story. It was July 29, 2012 when I arrived at The Citadel with my parents. I was wearing a light-blue shirt, khaki shorts, and a pair of tennis shoes. After arriving through the gates, I stepped out of the car and moved my belongings from the back seat to the curb. From there, I proceeded to the line of about one hundred others who had lined up on the concrete, which was painted in red-and-white squares. Known as *the quad*, a similar red-and-white checkerboard sprawls across the center of every battalion. As I approached, I noticed that nobody was talking, but then, as soon as I stepped onto the quad I heard this witch cry: *Screech!* It sounded like a cat fight. I looked to my left and saw that the loud noise was being emitted from a blond-haired guy who looked like a female. As I walked closer I realized that it was indeed a female, a girl.

"A girl? Girls go to The Citadel?"

"Yes. Actually, about ten percent of The Citadel Corps of Cadets is made up of girls. Most of them play soccer, volleyball, run track, or are there to commission into the military."

"Do you think I could go to The Citadel?" my seatmate asked.

"Let me tell you something my father told me," I said, smiling. "You can do anything you put your mind to. If you really wanted to, you could be the first female athlete to be the regimental commander at The Citadel."

"What's the regimental commander?"

"I'll get to that later in the story. Anyway, where was I… ah yes, being yelled at in line. My buddy Ty was standing in line behind me. I waved to him. He had a huge smile on his face and I saw he was wearing a blue Marilyn Monroe t-shirt that said *Good times with bad girls*."

"That's not an appropriate shirt to wear at a military college, is it?"

"No, it isn't… at least not for the first day. Do you watch Animal Planet?" I asked, and she nodded. "Have you ever seen how fast piranhas attack bloody meat in the water? Let's just say my buddy Ty was the meat and members of the female cadre were the piranhas all in his face yelling at the top of their lungs. I guess they didn't appreciate his shirt or his sense of humor."

I stood in line for what felt like an hour. By the time I reached the blue table where two upperclassmen cadets were handling registration, my shirt was completely drenched in sweat. It was Mr. Smith and Mr. Muhammed. I knew these guys. I had met them over the summer at a couple parties that had been given for members of the incoming class. I felt exhilarated, ready to start my new life in these new surroundings, to make new friends, to become a man. When it came my turn to be registered I put my hand on the table and said, "Carson, what's up man?"

He looked me dead in my eyes, "It's Mr. Smith, cadre squad corporal to you, and you can get your dirty hands off my table." It took a couple of seconds for me to register what had just transpired. *Wait a minute*, I thought, *isn't this the same guy I had seen at a couple of parties over the summer?* He had seemed like such a cool guy at the time. Obviously, he was a different person in uniform, a real-life Dr. Jekyll and Mr. Hyde. At the flip of a switch my cool teammate had transformed into Major Payne barking orders at us like we were his.... I won't say the word to you, but let's just say every member of the cadre was a pain in my behind.

As soon as I got my room number Mr. Muhammad said, "Crochet, you have five minutes to get your things, put them in your room, and say goodbye to your family." I so much wanted to say "Try me," but decided it would be best not to push my luck, especially on my first day. I hurried to my family outside of First Battalion, gave them a hug, and grabbed my things. "Well, this is going to be fun," I said to my mom as I hugged her goodbye. Having a sense of humor goes a long way, and trust me, it helps out a ton in this atmosphere.

I bounded up to my room. My roommate had already arrived. He was wearing a red collared shirt, khaki shorts, white socks, and tennis shoes, and he wore glasses.

"What's up, man? I'm Joe Crochet. How's it going?" I said and held out my hand.

"Hey man, my name is Chris. Need any help unpacking?"

Before I could respond, the loud screaming voice of one of the cadre filled the air. "Cadet recruits, you have two minutes till you need to be on the quad."

I looked over at Chris, who had already unpacked all his stuff and made his bed. He was comfortably sitting in his chair, reading from a small book that had something to do with The Citadel, or at least it looked that way from the cover. I asked him what he was reading.

"I am reading *The Guidon*," he said without taking his eyes off the book.

"The Guide… what? "

"*The Guidon*, you know the book you received in the mail. The one that you were supposed to study before starting Hell Week. It's our one source of information that contains everything we need to know about knob year, The Citadel, and guidelines on how to be successful here."

Oh, crap! Now, dear reader, if you read the introduction, you know that I love my family to death, but sometimes we have so much going on that the small items such as this book are not a high priority. Just knowing how my family operates, there was a great chance that this book, *The Guidon*, came in the mail a month ago, was put aside, and lost somewhere under piles of newspaper in the house.

"So, Chris, are you sure that I was supposed to have received a *Guidon* in the mail?"

"Yeah, man; you don't have one?" The obvious answer just by the inflection in my voice when I asked the question should have indicated the answer. The truth is, not only did I not have the book, but I had not even heard of it until that moment. "Dang, well—I'm sure you can get it at the cadet store or book store. Don't worry, man; you'll be all right."

Not a great way to start my new life at The Citadel.

Suddenly Mr. Smith barged into our room. Screaming. "Cadet recruits! Get your asses on the quad—now!" Chris about jumped out of his seat like a missile going to the moon. I thought he was going to hit his head on the ceiling. I dropped whatever was in my hand and we bolted out to the quad as fast as we could. All the fall sport athletes and managers were already lined up. Mr. German, the cadre commander and highest-ranking officer in the cadre, stood at the head. (Mr.

German, a six-foot-three, two-hundred-and-five-pound man, does not take any crap from anyone.)

First we had to march to the cadet store to get our uniforms, which meant being sized and fitted into all our different uniforms and shoes. (If you want to know a great business idea, it's being a uniform manufacturing company for military colleges. There will always be a high demand for them with the steady stream of students wanting to attend prestigious military colleges. They must mark those prices way up, too. I'm just happy to be on a full scholarship, because I know my parents would be aghast if they saw the price of my gray wool coat.)

As we walked from First Battalion to the cadet store, the only sounds were those of our feet hitting the hard asphalt and the cadre sounding off a cadence: *left, left, left, right, right, right, right, left.* When we arrived at the cadet store we were given our student IDs and told we had thirty minutes to gather our mandatory items before heading back to the barracks: PT pants, shirts, shorts, sweat pants, sweat shirts, reflector belt, knobby hat, ACU pants, ACU blouse, military boots, duty shirts, duty pants, black shoes, summer leave shirt, and summer leave pants. I had never shopped for new uniform clothes before. My mom always took my brother and me to a second-hand shop for our Catholic school uniforms. Therefore, I was quite shocked when I saw the total price of my new attire: $2,200. I handed my student ID to the cashier and said, "Thank God I'm not paying for this. My dad would kill me."

We returned to the barracks with our purchases. "Knobs, change into your PT uniforms and meet back on the quad in two minutes," a member of the cadre barked at us. Chris and I rushed back to our room and changed quickly. At this point I was telling myself, *This is not too bad. I still have my hair, and we haven't done anything too hard.* Unfortunately, I spoke too soon. Our next stop was the barbershop!

"Say goodbye to that pretty hair," one of the female cadre members said. I don't know why, but she gave me the impression that she hated guys, especially guys that looked like they cared about their personal appearance, like I did. We lined up in front of the gift shop in Mark Clark Hall and waited our turn to be shaved. *These barbers have it easy,* I thought as I stood there. *They only have to cut one hairstyle, and that hairstyle is bald.*

My hair was cut by a guy who goes by the nickname Shaky Willy. (Supposedly he's good at cutting hair unevenly.) At this point, I gave up caring about my personal appearance. I knew I was going to be bald for the next ten months, and it was a sacrifice I was willing to make. I was now a knob.

Freshly shaven, we gathered back in the hall to read our *Guidon.* Only one small problem…I didn't have one. Everyone stood in line with their *Guidons* held straight in front of their faces. Reading aloud, they chanted, "Oh Citadel, we sing thy fame for all the world to hear." I tuned them out, staring at the palm of my hand in front of my face, pretending it was a *Guidon,* pretending to know what I was supposed to say. I felt like an idiot standing there looking at my left hand. To make matters worse, my parents walked in through the front door right at that moment. Instead of leaving right away, they had decided to stop in the book store for some shirts and snacks for the ride back to Georgia.

My dad and I made eye contact. It took him a moment to recognize me—his own son of eighteen years—with my head as white as a newborn baby's ass that has been doused in baby powder. I so much wanted to tell him to get me the hell out of there. Instead, I bit my tongue and continued the farce of acting like I knew the words, like I had the *Guidon* in front of me. On the way out of the bookstore, my dad took his phone out and snapped a picture of me lined up looking at my hands. As they continued on their way, I thought: *Welcome to The Citadel.*

"Not everything happens when you want it to. It'll happen when the time is right. Be patient and trust the process."

- ANONYMOUS

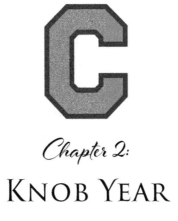

Chapter 2:

KNOB YEAR

A room in the barracks is not luxurious, but it is comfortable. The walls are painted light blue, the ceiling is white, and the floors are hardwood. In addition to the beds, each room contains two desks, two chairs, two full presses, two half presses, a medicine cabinet with a mirror, a sink, and two towel racks. Not much, but suitable for being my home for the next few years. In the summertime, the air conditioning barely works and in the wintertime the room stays chilly, with only a single vent in the ceiling for climate control. I am just glad it has that technology of HVAC, because before the 1980s, the barracks didn't yet have air conditioning or heating systems. Man, talk about the old corps!

As the sky darkened on our first evening there, members of the cadre confiscated our phones, laptops, watches, and alarm clocks to prevent us from communicating with the outside world and to ensure that we wouldn't know what time it was, night or day. It was meant to be a mind game. My first piece of advice for new cadets is this: Recognize that the entire knob year is a mind game. If you take it seriously, it can easily get to you, but if you know it's a mind game and remind yourself that it won't last forever, then you'll be able to make it through. Being able to establish priorities and set goals helped me through knob year and gave me a sense of purpose. Academics was my most important priority. I was not going to let knob year or football affect my grade point average. No matter what your viewpoint is of attending The Citadel, remember that, first and foremost, it is a college. I was there to get an education. Playing football and being a cadet were secondary to that fact. I set a short-term goal of getting a 4.0 GPA for my first semester.

During the first couple weeks of classes, I met with my TAC officer, Lieutenant Colonel Jefferson Panton. He wanted to counsel the knobs and help them set short term goals for themselves. I knocked on his door. "Sir, Lieutenant Colonel Panton, sir. Cadet recruit Crochet would like permission to enter your room sir."

"Drive in, Crotchet." (It took him at least two years before he properly pronounced my last name.) I took a seat, sweating like a whore in church, intimidated by the vast number of awards and medals adorning his office. The rumor around the battalion was that Lieutenant Colonel Panton had a confirmed kill with a shovel. I've heard some crazy war stories, but a killing with a shovel tops my list. As it was our first meeting, Panton first needed to get the basics: Hometown, height and weight, high school GPA, sports? As soon as I told him I was on the football team, he looked me straight in the eye and said, "Corps Squad... Crotchet, you need to understand that there's a divide between the Corps and the Corps Squad. I know how much stuff you guys go through on a daily basis, but these other cats have no idea what you're going through. They think you're skipping out on mandatory knob duties when you go to practice, workouts, meetings, or traveling for games. Just promise me that you'll do your due diligence and be at everything you can make. I've also talked with Weaver and Goins about this, and I think that you three can help change the bad stigma around here."

"Yes sir." I didn't know what else I could say. All I could think about was the fact that I was talking to a man who might have the ability to take someone out with a shovel. That's the most bad-ass story I'd ever heard. Coming from a military family where both my uncles were airborne rangers and colonels in the United States Army, I was accustomed to military talk, but never did I think I would be at a military institution, bald as a doorknob, conversing with a prestigious man who would mentor me throughout my cadet life.

My second piece of advice for anyone hoping to survive knob year is to establish and adhere to a routine. After Hell Week, I made a point to set my schedule. The first semester of college was underway. Every morning I woke up at 5:40 a.m., participated in sweep detail, then Kyle, Trey, Caleb, and I walked to the gym in Seignious Hall for a light workout, then had time to shower, and be back in the barracks by 7:05 a.m. for breakfast formation. It's important to start your day off strong and get your blood flowing. The most successful people in the world make a point to do more in their morning than the average person will do in his or her entire day.

It was great to get away from the craziness inside the barracks; however, returning was never fun. Every time we walked back from Seignious Hall, at least one upperclassman tried to get us into trouble. However, Trey, Kyle, Caleb, Eric, and I had our morning routine down and as long as we just looked straight ahead, kept a hundred and twenty-pace walk, and "sir-sandwiched" seniors while saluting officers we were in the clear.

"What's a sir sandwich?" asked my interlocutor, still paying attention, still rapt with my story.

"It's when we as cadets say, sir whatever we have to say, sir. Just imagine the sir at the beginning and end of a statement is like bread on a sandwich. The meat and condiments are what comes in between."

"Oh, I thought it was an actual sandwich."

"Oh no, but that would be one heck of a name for a sandwich. The Citadel Canteen should make a sandwich like that. It could also replace the name for the chicken ho-ah, the famous Citadel chicken sandwich that I'll tell you about in just a minute. Ok…where was I?"

Oh, yes…it took a while to get into our morning routine. We started off leaving the locker room at 6:50 a.m., but quickly realized that we would be the first ones lined up on the side sally ports in Law Barracks, where we would be fresh meat for the hungry wolves. What I mean is that it was the role of upperclassmen to give us knobs a hard time. They would confront us for having imperfect creases in our shirts or randomly demand that we do twenty-five push-ups for no other reason than to take out their own aggressions on someone. One bright morning, we came up with the clever idea of leaving Seignious Hall a little later. Doing so would mean there'd be less of a chance we'd get racked out by upperclassmen but still have enough time to get to morning formation. Remember, knob year is a game. Twenty years from now, nobody is going to talk about how great of a knob you were. All they're going to talk about is whether or not you made it through knob year and graduated from The Citadel. Like anything in life, there are ways to properly play by the rules, but still have an advantage in areas that are not specifically defined. I knew from the beginning that in order to thrive during knob year, I needed to team up with other knobs in my company and battalion and figure out the loopholes within the rules to make sure I could successfully play the game. My mindset was to slowly chip away at knob year by taking it one day at a time. Isn't that what my dad meant when he said: *The only way to eat an elephant is one bite at a time?*

You have to play the game in order to be successful at The Citadel. Coach Larkins, the special teams' coordinator and linebackers' coach, described it as flipping the switch. For instance, when you walk in and out of a room, you flip the switch to turn on or off the light. At football practice, football is all that mattered. All the other distractions within the Corps, academics, friends, family, and any other issues were of no concern during that time. The moment I walked through Seignious Hall's doors my main focus became football, and that is the switch I had to turn on at practice, during film, at workouts, and especially on game day. Inside the barracks and outside walking around campus, I had to turn on my cadet switch. Inside the academic buildings I had to turn on my academic switch. It's all about having the mindset to be the best you can be at whatever it is you are doing at the moment. This all starts with focus.

As long as our uniform, personal appearance and room presentation met Citadel standards and we were on time to everything, there was no way we could get in trouble. Shoes and belt brass needed to be shined, duty shirt needed to be ironed with military creases, and backing had to be used behind our name tags to make them flush with our shirts; in addition, the L pin for Lima Company and the four pin for fourth class system had to be placed perfectly parallel with the collar.

Knob year is all about prioritizing. In addition to knob knowledge, the information inside of the *Guidon* that every knob should know, it's important to know about opportunity costs and to distinguish between what's important and what's a waste of time. I learned the Alma Mater, the Cadet Prayer, and the Cadet Creed. All the other knob knowledge I would just pretend to sound off, mouthing out my x's and o's, looking straight ahead, and hoping an upperclassman was not going to call me out for not knowing the knob knowledge.

THE CITADEL ALMA MATER (1943)

Oh Citadel, we sing thy fame
For all the world to hear.
And in the Paths our fathers showed us
Follow without fear.
Peace and Honor, God and Country,
We will fight for thee.
Oh Citadel, we praise thee now
And in Eternity.
Oh Citadel, though strife surrounds us,
We will ever be
Full conscious of the benefits
That we derive from thee.
Stand forever, yielding never
To the tyrant's Hell
We'll never cease our struggles for
Our mighty Citadel.

(Cadet A. Preston Price, '43)

THE CITADEL CADET CREED

"I will always endeavor to uphold the prestige, honor, and high *esprit de corps* of The Citadel and The South Carolina Corps of Cadets. Never shall I fail my comrades. I will always keep myself mentally alert, physically tough, and morally straight, and I will shoulder more than my share of the task whatever it may be. Gallantly will I show the world that I am a well- trained cadet. My courtesy to superior officers, neatness of dress, and care of equipment shall set the example for others to follow. And under no circumstances will I ever bring discredit to The Citadel and The South Carolina Corps of Cadets."

BG James E. Mace
USA, Ret., '63 Adapted from
U.S. Army Rangers 75th Infantry Regiment

THE CADET PRAYER

Almighty God, the source of light and strength, we implore Thy blessing on this our beloved institution, that it may continue true to its high purposes.

Guide and strengthen those upon whom rests the authority of government; enlighten with wisdom those who teach and those who learn; and grant to all of us that through sound learning and firm leadership, we may prove ourselves worthy citizens of our country, devoted to truth, given to unselfish service, loyal to every obligation of life and above all to Thee.

Preserve us faithful to the ideals of The Citadel, sincere in fellowship, unswerving in duty, finding joy in purity, and confidence through a steadfast faith.

Grant to each one of us, in his (her) own life, a humble heart, a steadfast purpose, and a joyful hope, with a readiness to endure hardship and suffer if need be, that truth may prevail among us and that Thy will may be done on earth. Through Jesus Christ, our Lord. Amen.

Bishop Albert S. Thomas, Ret.,
First Honor Graduate
Class of 1892

My fourth piece of advice for thriving during your knob year is to use every resource and opportunity you have to stay out of the barracks. In the barracks, upperclassmen can and will walk into your room at any time. Their job is to humiliate, to scold, to make your life a living hell. Fortunately, I had football workouts, meetings, and mandatory practices every day after my afternoon classes. After practice, I would go to the Academic Support Center in Thompson Hall and partake in study hall from 7:50 p.m. till closing at 10:00 p.m. The Academic Support Center is available to every cadet and is a great resource to utilize throughout your career there. Going to the library is another solution for getting out of the barracks. I did my best to avoid the upperclassmen and focus on academics, working toward my goal of getting a 4.0 GPA.

Though the upperclassmen on campus went out of their way to make our lives miserable, in the locker room, everyone was equal. Some of them even did everything possible to help the freshmen (when it came to football, that is). Some of the upperclassmen looked out for us, inviting us knobs to their off-campus apartments during general leave, thereby helping us get our minds off the stress of being knobs, and providing us with advice and guidance. True mentors. Others, however, couldn't have cared less.

A war was being waged inside Lesesne Gates. The culture of the team during the time was poor and there was a divide between the coaching staff and the players. The chasm between the regular Corps of Cadets and the Corps Squad was at an all-time high. Not a good recipe for a successful season. With the football program traditionally not being that good and the regular Corps and TAC officers singling out cadet athletes, it was not a great environment to be in during knob year. I would put on my intimidating face whenever I stepped out, walking a hundred and twenty steps per minute on campus or in the barracks on the way to my room. Most of the upperclassmen didn't mess with me too much, but some of them made it a point to go out of their way to pick on me, Kyle, and Eric. This situation lasted for months, but it felt like an eternity.

"So, did you ever want to hit an upperclassman?"

Looking at Mary, I couldn't help but smile. "I like your passion, and please believe me, I wanted to fight some of them every time I saw them; however, that is not how you win the game."

"But they were so mean to you, though."

"Well, that's because people hate what they fear and fear what they don't know. I can't hate someone for treating me like crap. I just feel sorry for them because they think that treating someone like that is okay. They're the ones who must live with the way they are. I just simply forgive and forget."

Anyway, where was I... oh, yes. To help pass the time, our classmates would make sure to have a great time on the weekends and whenever we had general leave. I mean, for crying out loud, we were living in the number one city in the world! I wish the girls thought our cadet uniforms were more attractive, though. Ever since World War II, our uniforms did not have the right effect on college girls—at least not on college girls at the neighboring liberal arts school, The College of Charleston. Many of its student body were not impressed with the more reserved and conservative environment of the military. Well, that went for Freshman and Sophomore year. Once, a cadet is an upperclassmen the College of Charleston girls start to take a huge liking toward Citadel cadets.

Ah... I almost forgot to mention... one other thing we had to pass the time were friendly competitions. We had basketball games, two-hand touch football, and racquetball. But the most memorable of all was the wrestling match between me and Caleb. At this point our football season had ended, so the coaches didn't care if we got hurt or not, and we had a bit of free time as the semester was almost complete—the only thing remaining to do was to prepare for exams. It was the perfect opportunity for a wrestling death match.

The month leading up to the fight was the most fun aspect of it all. We did phone interviews and Snap Chat videos with each other, and other such promotions to hype it. Imagine a small-scale Conner McGregor and Floyd Mayweather fight. People were betting on who was going to win. It got so competitive that people hyped us up in the mess hall, trying to spark up a reaction. There had never been—nor will there ever be—another wrestling showdown at The Citadel equivalent to the one that was about to unfold.

Caleb had the advantage with Preston, a former South Carolina high-school all-state wrestler, as his coach. Preston knew the proper technique to take people down. He even taught Caleb wrestling moves to use for the match. As for me, I was going into it blind. I knew that our strengths were matched, but I was definitely the more athletic of the two of us. It was hubris on my part to think there was no way for him to win—as long as he didn't get behind me, that is.

The wrestling match took place inside Vandiver Hall on the actual wresting team's practice mats. Undisclosed to the wrestling team or coaches, we were, in reality, trespassing. Every knob on our football team, as well as a couple of upperclassmen, gathered to watch. A loud roar of cheering greeted us as we walked in to take our places on the mat. It felt like I was lining up for kickoff in Johnson Hagood Memorial Stadium. My adrenaline was pumping, and I felt amazing.

As we faced each other on the mat, I noticed that Caleb looked determined, and I could sense this would be one to remember. From all sides, our supporters yelled out words of encouragement: "Get him, Joe." "Show that pretty boy who's boss, Caleb."

The rules of engagement were that everything except punching and kicking was fair game and that the winner would be declared by either a tap-out, pin, knock-out, or first draw of blood.

I had a game plan for taking Caleb down, which was no doubt similar to his own plan for victory. I wanted to get his legs, tackle him, or get behind him to slam him to the ground. I took a few deep breaths, waiting for the bell to indicate the match should begin.

We both started circling the ring, waiting for the other to make the first move. Wrestling is a game of strategy, and like any chess match, the first one to make a move is not always the first one to call checkmate. Caleb made the first move by trying to grab my leg. I moved swiftly out of the way and tried countering his attack and then… crap, he got me in a headlock.

"Thatta boy, Caleb!" Preston yelled from his corner. The crowd started yelling even louder, because they thought I was about to get pinned. Caleb began squeezing my neck, waiting for me to tap out or something. I could barely breathe. I thought I was going to pass out, but by some luck, I was able to grab Caleb's entire body, lift him up, and slam him to the ground.

You know those stories about how people during life-or-death situations develop supernatural strength… well, that shit kicked in and oh, did I need it! As soon as he hit the mat, he released me from the headlock. As he was lying on the ground trying to get up, I jumped behind him, grabbed him, and (wham) slammed him into the mat again. Caleb's nose started bleeding. I won the match! I could hear the crowd going crazy all around: *Hell yeah, Joe; That's how you do the damn thing! Caleb, are you kidding me?* Winning is sweet. All of my teammates stormed the mat as if we just beat Charleston Southern in Johnson Hagood Stadium. My heart was swelling with the pride of victory.

"What the hell are y'all doing on my practice mat?" It was the head wrestling coach. He had just walked in on us. The crowd scattered like baby spiders hatching from an egg. As soon as the coach walked in... we all ran. Well, everyone, that is, except me and Caleb.

After a long talking-to by the head wrestling coach and Coach Higgins, head football coach, we had learned our lesson. I realize now that we could have gotten seriously hurt or—even worse—hurt someone else. But still, I think it was worth it. Doing something fun like that created a unique family spirit in our class. I swear we have the closest class out of any class that has ever gone, or will ever go, through The Citadel.

The rest of the time flew by after that. We made it through exams and I finished the semester with a 4.0 GPA. I had achieved my semester academic goal, and now it was time to relax on Christmas break. Those two weeks back home were so precious. I could eat whatever I wanted, hang out with my family and friends. In all honesty, I didn't want to leave to go back to Charleston, but I had a job to do.

The following semester, however, didn't go by as fast—at least not at first. Being at The Citadel in January was pretty boring; the weather was cold and crappy, and the nights were dark and long. We had workouts every single day. However, as soon as it started warming up (which it does as early as February in Charleston) morale started to improve. The rest of the semester flew by: spring practice, then spring break and Easter break. We went to the beach every weekend after that. It was a great time to be in Charleston. Now the only event stopping us from completing knob year was Recognition Day.

Recognition Day, also known as Rec Day, is the second-best day of a cadet's life.

"What's the first best day?"

"Graduation! But I'll tell you about that later. I can't skip the entire journey on getting there. Just hold your horses a little and I will eventually get there."

So anyway, back to Rec Day. The night before Rec Day is nerve-wracking. All the upperclassmen cadets only have one more night and a day to vent their frustrations on knobs. As soon as the clock strikes one o'clock the following afternoon, knobs would no longer be scapegoats for them. As Chris and I were preparing our things for the next day, we heard a light knock on the door. It was the regimental commander. Stunned in disbelief, Chris and I just stood there in room attention. As the regimental commander came into the room, he reached out his hand to shake mine.

"Hi, I'm Patrick," he said.

Did he just introduce himself to me, a mere knob, by his first name? At The Citadel knobs do not have the privilege of knowing upperclassmen's' first names. Stunned, I shook his hand. "Hi, I'm Joe," I murmured. He shook Chris's hand as well. He treated both of us as actual human beings. This was the first time an upperclassman cadet outside of my teammates had recognized me for me and not just called me by my last name. It was liberating to finally be recognized as a human being instead of as a knob by an upperclassman cadet—and not just any upperclassman cadet, but the highest-ranking cadet in the Corps! I know now that it's tradition for the regimental commander to recognize all the knobs the day before Rec Day. Only one day remaining until I no longer was a knob. Ah, Rec Day....

That night I fell fast asleep on the top bunk dreaming about being done with knob year. Suddenly, I woke up to the sound of the lock on the door being unlocked. From the bunk below, I heard Chris snoring louder than ever.

"Chris!" I yelled.

"What, dude?" he said, startled awake.

"I think it's happening."

We both bolted out of bed and hurried to change into our personal training attire. The day we'd been waiting for since we matriculated was about to commence, and we weren't sure what to expect. None of the upperclassmen on the team would tell us anything about this day except that it wasn't hard. "All you have to do are some pushups and a run around campus," they said. I knew this was a load of you-know-what. I knew it would be a challenge. Chris, Kyle, Eric, Caleb, Trey, and all our brothers from the class of 2016 were mentally prepared.

The night before, the sophomores had taped up our phones, watches, and laptops so I didn't know what time it was. All I knew was that it was early Saturday morning. Chris and I got dressed in our PTs and waited for the inevitable to happen.

"What are PTs?" my young listener asked.

"PTs are The Citadel's mandatory uniform for exercising, basically gym shorts and shirts with a reflector belt. We had to wear them whenever we were doing physical activity outside."

It was only a few moments later that our door got kicked open and we were greeted by the stern faces of three upperclassmen screaming at the top of their lungs at us to line up for morning PT, their spit flying all over our faces. They seemed surprised to see us already up and dressed. After such a pleasant good morning from our upperclassmen, Chris and I filled our CamelBaks and proceeded as instructed.

On the side sally port, we lined up in an orderly fashion. From there, we did hundreds of flutter kicks, push-ups, and many other exercises. Normally, these exercises would not have been that tough, but we were doing everything with continuous movement. When we are not doing stationary exercises, we had to high knee in place, raising our hands above our shoulders and making the sign of an L with our fingers. We had a cadence chanting, "We love (clap-clap) Lima" for at least an hour. After that, we ran on to the parade deck, Summerall field, and for about forty-five minutes we did more stationary physical training. I swear we did at least a thousand flutter kicks and push-ups. Once that was over, we went on the spirit run. The spirit run is a three- to four-mile run around campus. That was tough for me at the time. At two-hundred-and-twenty pounds, I was not used to running long distances, but I knew I wasn't struggling as much as the two-hundred-and-ninety-pound football players. During the run, they made us sound off to a bunch of cadences and chant *We love Lima* over a thousand times. By the time we entered the Third Battalion toward the end of the route, I was exhausted. We ran around in a huge circle on the quad about ten times. As we circled the quad, I could feel the salt on my body start to accumulate from all the sweat. As soon as the run ended we shot over to the sally port to do an insane number of push-ups.

"This is just the warm-up," an upperclassman cadet reminded us. "Okay. Good work, cadets. You have three minutes to shower, change, and be back down here on the quad." We jetted up to the fourth division to go shower.

After the shower, we changed into our army combat uniforms (ACUs) and returned to formation. I felt like a boss wearing an ACU and combat boots. It gave me such a sense of pride. I mean, it goes without saying, just look at it: It's the uniform of the best military in world. Anyway, back to the story… I ran downstairs, and just as I lined up in formation: "Cadets y'all know what time it is…." An upperclassman cadet walked onto the quad, threw down his hat, and started doing push-ups. We had to follow his lead. We started cranking them out. By this time, I could see my parents peeking their heads through the front sally port. I know they, along with so many other parents, were so proud of their child being able to accomplish this great feat. It was a monumental day for me, but an even bigger day for my family.

After doing another insane number of push-ups and flutter kicks, we formed up and marched over to the mess hall for breakfast. Finally, a break! I know football games are tiring, but at least you get three timeouts each half. What they were doing to us was damn near cruel. We lined up in front of the mess hall, and from there we filed off from the right into the building. The weird thing about every movement was that we had to sound off with our ditties and had to race everywhere we went. It was like Hell Week all over again, but I truly didn't care. They could have tortured me that day, just as long as it was my last day being a knob. Only a couple more hours until I would have my freedom back—a freedom that had been taken away from me ten months ago.

At breakfast we were forced to perch on the front three inches of our chairs. I had to ask permission from our mess carver before grabbing a food item and drink. Another rule at the dining table is you can't backhand your neighbor, which means that every knob must pass food to his or her neighbor with the farther hand. It's simple rules of etiquette like this that distinguish Citadel cadets from normal students. Another rule at the table is that we had to face forward and could not chew until our forks were put down.

The mess carver at my table was Mr. Aguero, a sinister kind of senior cadet. It was his mission to make this, out last meal as knobs, the most disgusting meal of our lives.

"Hey you," Aguero snarled, pointing to the knob seated next to me. "Do you like hot chocolate milk?"

"Sir, yes sir, Mr. Aguero. I love hot chocolate milk, sir."

Agueuro chuckled, "Well, since you love it so much, I want you to eat and drink this hot chocolate drink with hot sauce, chocolate milk, and mayonnaise for whip cream." He threw in a couple other condiments too. Technically, the cadet didn't have to do it. He could have gotten up and gone to the bathroom. I mean, we were still American citizens and had a right to choose what we would eat, but in honor of it being the last meal he would eat as a knob, it seemed like more of a privilege to do so. I mean Agueuro had called him out, so what was he going to do... say no? Not on the last day. I joined him in on it as well. It was horrible-tasting, of course, so I just kept thinking to myself that I was doing it for the class of 2016 and that helped me get it down. At least I didn't have to eat unpeeled bananas like those at the next table were called on to do.

The main course for the final knob meal was chicken biscuits. Unfortunately, they looked nothing like Chick-fil-a's famous breakfast meal; rather, they looked like a science project. Well, that is, after Mr. Aguero suggested his choice of condiments, which I'm sure you can only imagine were disgusting. As I was eating this delightful breakfast... it happened. My stomach started turning. I looked around the table thinking, *Shit... am I really about to puke?* Luckily for me, I wasn't the only one feeling that way. The three knobs next to me started puking all over their plates and the table, making me want to retch even more. *Hold it in, Joe; hold it in,* I told myself and kept facing forward, trying not to hear the sounds of their retching.

We'd only been in the mess hall for about ten minutes, but it felt like an eternity.

After the "hell meal," we lined up again and marched to Duckett Hall, where we had an hour-long meeting with our current and future battalion commanders. They reflected on our knob year and outlined expectations for our post-knob Citadel experience. Man, the post-knob experience sounded amazing. Only a couple more hours, and I'd be free! After our battalion meeting, I gathered with my company in our classroom in Bond Hall for more reflection and outlining of expectations, this time from our current and future company commanders. The future sounded so bright. Excitement overpowered my exhaustion.

After the meetings were over, however, the true hell on earth began.

We formed up directly outside the steps of Bond Hall and marched back to the battalion. By this time, many families and friends had gathered around campus to watch us on our final day as knobs. I spotted my dad in several places. He had been there since 5 a.m. and followed us like white on rice. We marched into Law Barracks and stopped at the large L, our company letter, on the quad. An upperclassman yelled, "Knobs, go to your rooms and grab a towel. Once you do this, get your asses down here ASAP and then form back up on line." I sprinted to my room, thinking that if I were the first one to my room, then I would get a longer break before having to be back on line. Unfortunately, I was wrong. As soon as I closed the door to my room, (kick) an upperclassman barged in demanding that I get downstairs…go, go, go!

I lined back up on the quad only to do more stationary physical training. After today, I thought, my waist would be at least four inches smaller. Between the flutter kicks, sit-ups, push-ups, and other stationary drills, I was lost in the moment. *Only two more hours until freedom…only two more hours…* I kept thinking to myself.

"All right, knobs, form up," our company commander demanded. "Grab your things and let's head out." We sprint-marched to the soccer field. The Gauntlet—the hardest part of Recognition Day—was about to begin. Parents, friends, coaches, upperclassmen, and everyone else on campus gathered around the field. There had to be at least five thousand friends and families watching the class of 2016 enter the Gauntlet. I spotted my mom and dad on the outskirts as we entered. Man, was I happy to see them.

The Gauntlet is set up as a cross-fit and military drill course with one hundred and twelve stations. By this time the humidity was kicking in. The field was muddy and wet from rain the day before. The bugs were out, and I knew it was going to be an event I would never forget.

We started off doing partner runs, partner bear crawls, low crawls, high crawls, and more bear crawls. The partner bear crawls were the worst station because Kyle was my partner, and he weighed a hell of a lot more than I did.

(Whistle blew) "Knobs, change stations."

I left the bear crawls to head over to the sand bag walks and lunges. At this point, I could barely feel my legs. They were heavier than anything I had ever felt before.

(Whistle blew) "Next station, knobs."

As we moved to the next group of exercises, all I could focus on were the parents and friends cheering us on. Their energy gave me energy. It was quite an amazing feeling. The next stage was the combat rolls and prowlers.

Thank God for Coach D—Donnell Boucher—and his off-season workouts. I would have been completely out of shape if it weren't for him and his strength staff. After prowlers, we ran over to do jumping jacks, up-downs, flutter kicks, push-ups, and pilates. This was where my body started fatiguing on me. I was in the middle of jumping jacks when my left leg went into a full leg cramp. Andy, the head athletic trainer, rushed over with a Powerade. "Here you go, drink this, wait a bit to let your body rehydrate itself, and then go out and finish the damn thing." He was not one for sympathy, and I was not one to quit.

I got up and finished my jumping jacks. My body was feeling much better after that quick shot of Powerade. The rest of the Gauntlet consisted of log sit-ups, log shoulder raises, weight shoulder presses, and many other stations. To me the hardest station by far was the human tunnel station. For an entire seven minutes we held ourselves up creating an arch so that our classmates could crawl underneath us. "Come on, knobs, do not abandon your classmates." This was the longest plank I ever had held. I looked over at Eric and Kyle, and all three of us gave each other the look that we got this. I couldn't fail, especially on them. If they could hold it up, I needed to suck up the pain and do so, too. It was the longest seven minutes of my life.

(Whistle blew) "Knobs, great job. Get some water and then form up, though we are done with the Gauntlet, we still aren't done." The Gauntlet had been conquered; however, there were a couple missions left to complete this cycle of being recognized.

After the Gauntlet, we formed up on the field for our final time as knobs, family and friends cheering us on as we left the field to prepare for the victory lap. The victory lap consists of a two-mile run around campus in our ACUs and boots. It's the very last step in accomplishing this heavy milestone. I was extremely exhausted; Both of my legs were cramping. But I knew I had to do it. I couldn't come this far just to give up. I needed to not only finish but to be up in the front with my classmates. I had never run a faster two miles in my entire life. Jacked up on adrenaline, I was lighter than ever before because of all the sweat I had lost throughout the day. We breezed through those two miles as if our lives depended on it. As we made the final bend, all my nerves and excitement could not be held within. The only thing that stood between me and not being a knob anymore was a 250-yard sprint and a class set of a hundred and sixteen push-ups.

My adrenaline and epinephrine were at an all-time high. I truly was high on life and it was driving me to a state where I felt like Superman. I sprinted those last two hundred and fifty yards. At that point I didn't care about the cramps or the fact that I had probably lost twenty-five pounds of water. As we were sprinting in front of the battalions, I saw my family. They were so happy. Everything from the moment of them dropping me off at The Citadel, to getting my head shaved, to all of the knob stories that had happened in between—it was all about to finally end.

I started to pump up my classmates, jumping up and down, screaming at the top of my lungs: "We love (clap-clap) Lima." As we entered the battalion, I started high-stepping, bumping into everyone. Suddenly everyone started getting more and more excited. The realization that all the bullshit was finally about to be over crept into their minds. I felt like I was about to play a football game in overtime. We ran into the battalion and formed a huge circle around our company letter "L" with our mentors.

"Knobs, it's time for the final stage in completing the process of knob year," said our company commander.

My senior mentor was D-Rob, fullback on The Citadel football team and upperclassman in Lima Company. He looked me in the eyes. "Joe Cro, you got this!" All I had to do was one hundred and sixteen push-ups and then my initiation process into The Citadel would be complete. D-Rob had with him a white towel which could be used to assist me with my class set (one hundred sixteen push-ups since we were the class of '16) because there was no way I was going to be able to do one hundred sixteen push-ups by myself, especially after everything we had just done. However, that was not my mindset. I wanted to try get one hundred sixteen push-ups without stopping or without help. D-Rob insisted, however, and I dropped to the floor with the towel. "One, two, three, four…." D-Rob kept counting as I kept pushing. "Forty, forty-one, forty-two, forty-three …." I could feel the muscles in my arms and chest shaking and starting to cramp every time I locked out at the top of my push-up. "Sixty-one, sixty-two, sixty-three…." I was determined. "Seventy-four, seventy-five, seventy-six …." Suddenly, I could not push from the ground. I took a break lying on the quad. The entire time I could hear D-Rob and the other upperclassmen cheering me and my classmates on. "Joe Cro, get your ass up, man. You only have to do a couple more. Finish the damn thing." I pushed myself up. I had to finish. D-Rob made sure I kept going. "Eighty-one, eighty-two, eighty-three…." I was so close, yet finishing is the toughest part. "One hundred one, one hundred two, one hundred three… only thirteen more push-ups!" My adrenaline started to kick in again. "One hundred fourteen, one hundred fifteen …." Suddenly I felt D-Rob let go of the towel and I fell to my chest. D-Rob said, "Joe, for this last one you're going to have to do it by yourself. You've been able to get this far on your own… now finish it." I was weak, tired, exhausted, and had every excuse in the book going through my mind; however, one thing I knew for sure –I was not going to quit.

"I cannot quit!" I yelled out.

D-Rob started clapping, "A hundred sixteen…that's how you do the damn thing, Joe."

I collapsed on the red-and-white-checkered concrete. I had done it. D-Rob grabbed the CamelBak from my back. "Stay on the ground, Joe Cro, and relax. You did good, man; you did good." He put the very towel he had used to assist me with push-ups over my head and dumped the water out of the CamelBak onto the towel. Chris and Kyle finished right after me. I was lying between both… exhausted.

We linked hands while lying there face down on that red-and-white-checkered board. We'd done it. The quad was such a nasty place to put your bare face on, but at that moment it felt like I was on a cloud. Man, I couldn't believe the hard part was finally over. After everyone in my company finished their class set, we were told to crawl and touch the Guidon, our company battle flag located in front of our company letter. I was one of the first people to get there, which consequently meant that I was at the bottom of the pile. We each put a hand on the Guidon. Tradition says that at this moment, every knob must recite the cadet prayer: "Almighty God, the source of light and strength, we implore Thy blessing on this our beloved institution, that it may continue true to its high purposes" … As we recited the prayer, I was in a state of amazement. We'd done it! "Guide and strengthen those upon whom rests the authority of government; enlighten with wisdom those who teach and those who learn; and grant to all of us that through sound learning…"

I couldn't see much, but I felt all the souls above and next to me. We together had done it. "Preserve us faithful to the ideals of The Citadel, sincere in fellowship, unswerving in duty … Thy will may be done on earth. Through Jesus Christ, our Lord. Amen."

As soon as we yelled *Amen*, over forty gallons of water fell on us. It was glorious. I soaked in the moment; all the bullshit was finally over. Afterward, we crawled to the big block letter L and kissed it. I would have made out with it if given the chance. We stood in a line and put our arms around each other, braced the hardest we had ever braced, and waited for the announcements over the intercom. Now, every company inside the battalion—Lima, India, Mike, and Kilo— were all doing the same thing. I saw my high school buddy Trey bracing like no one ever has. I saw Caleb doing the same thing. It was the final brace I would ever do. We braced for several minutes. Then it finally happened. The intercom came to life. "Good afternoon to The Citadel Corps of Cadets. This is your regimental commander." He followed his announcement with a speech about his excitement for our class and being honored to have been the regimental commander of this great institution. Finally, he congratulated all the knobs for having endured the year. He talked about the special achievement we had just completed and how monumental it was for our Citadel career. At the end of his speech he announced, "Ladies and gentlemen of the class of 2016, the fourth-class system is no longer in effect." Those words, the way they all flowed together, were the epitome of everything grammar is supposed to do. Such a release of emotion came over the entire school the moment he said those words. For those that believe words aren't powerful, I dare you to visit The Citadel when those very words are said aloud for the entire Charleston peninsula to hear. They were the sweetest words I had ever heard and probably ever will hear. This moment was one of the most powerful moments of my life.

Afterwards I ran over to hug my classmates. I gave Eric and Kyle a huge hug. "We did it, big Joe... we did it!" Kyle said, holding back tears. We then formed back up in a line to be recognized by the up-perclassmen. I went outside the battalion and gave my mom and dad a huge hug. We took a bunch of pictures. They were so proud. After pictures with Trey, Caleb, Kyle, Eric, and Chris, we then relaxed, eating burgers and chips on the quad.

At around 3:30 p.m., our entire class of 2016 changed into dress whites and marched to the old Citadel, which is now the Embassy Suites by Hilton in downtown Charleston. It's a Citadel tradition to parade through Charleston. Gathered out there in the middle of Marion Square, we were free. Standing on the lawn in front of the old Citadel was the presentation of the new regimental commander. After that, we marched back to The Citadel to change, and then we were free to spend time with our families.

I will remember 2013 Recognition Day forever. My mom filmed the entire event and my dad has pictures from 5:30 a.m. all the way up to our march to the old Citadel. I'm sure that the only reason he stopped taking photos was because he didn't have enough storage on his camera chip.

The Citadel is the only military college in the United States with a ten-month-long plebe year. Every other military college's plebe year is far less than ours, at a semester or even less. This is just one feature that distinguishes The Citadel from all other institutions in the country.

I looked out the window, reminiscing.

"Hey, Joe—what are you doing? Finish the story."

I turned to look at Mary. "Oh, I'm just thinking about that day."

Truly, looking back on it, I am so happy I took the challenge of taking the road less traveled. I wish good luck to anyone who decides to take this journey. It is not easy, but I have four words of advice coming from my experience: It is worth it!

"Is that it? Is that how you got your ring?"

"Oh no, little one, that was just the first step of the journey. There are more obstacles ahead before you hear how I got my ring. So, yes, we had just marched downtown and returned back to campus to change and spend time with our families. But then as we were collecting our things, the first rumor since being recognized started churning around the quad. One of my classmates said he had heard that sophomore year was worse than freshman year. I looked at him and, without hesitation, said, "I can't wait!" I gave him a thumbs-up and proceeded to enjoy the rest of my day. In the back of my mind I couldn't help but think: *How much worse can it be?*

"You are very attractive and your greatest charm is that you do not realize it!"

- A.J. CRONIN

YEAR TWO

Red-Shirt Freshman Season

Chapter 3:

MORE THAN PUPPY LOVE

On April 5, 2013, my world changed completely. It was the day I met "the one."

Of course, I didn't know it was going to happen when I woke up that morning, but I did know that it would be a special day. It was my cousin Patrick's birthday, and Kyle, Caleb, and I were driving to Clemson University to celebrate the occasion. Patrick was born three days before me at the same hospital. Maybe that's why we've always been so close.

It was about a four-hour ride and, let me tell you, we had a blast on the way. I strongly urge my readers to take a road trip with friends at least once in their lives. When we arrived at Clemson, around 9:00 p.m., we made our way to the Horseshoe Dorms, right next to Clemson Memorial Stadium. The Horseshoe is a coed dormitory that houses hundreds of naive and stimulated freshmen. As we walked into the dorm building, the smell of alcohol and weed had already met my senses. As a guy who has only drunk once in his life and has never done drugs, I was curious to see the college lifestyle first hand. Pat showed us up to his room where he had a pregame going on.

"What's a pregame?"

"A pregame is a get-together with friends before going out for the evening."

"What do you do at a pregame?"

"You'll learn about that when you're older," I said, glancing at Mary's mother. Who would have thought I would be talking to a little girl on a plane from a place I never thought I would go to and talking about my days partying in college? Anyway, I was just rolling with the path God has put me on.

In all fairness, the freshman dorms were not much better than the barracks. The quarters were small and had bunk beds, just like Third Battalion. We started drinking warm vodka. "Vodka? What's that?"

"An adult beverage. I'm sure your mommy has had it once or twice in her life," I said and noticed Mary's mom smiling in the seat beside her.

Although I'm not a huge fan of warm alcohol, these are the years to experience it, right? As a young, naive knob, I felt it was necessary to indulge in some harmless shenanigans. We finished the bottle in thirty minutes.

"Man, that wasn't too bad," Kyle said with a grimace.

I wondered how anyone could drink such a beverage on a regular basis and looked at Caleb to see his reaction. We were feeling good—buzzing and full of excitement for what the night would bring. More and more people were entering the room.

And that's when it happened. I turned my head and saw the most beautiful girl in the world enter the room. Actually, to say she entered the room is an understatement. She *lit up* the room is more like it. It seemed as if the entire room grew silent. She was wearing a pink tank top, blue jeans, and brown boots. She had a gorgeous white smile and her eyes were the color of a diamond: sky-blue forged from the clouds of heaven. Her hair was a luscious dark brown, flowing like the sea of life. I couldn't take my eyes off her. All the guys were staring at her like hungry dogs waiting for their owners to give them a steak. Everyone could see that she was physically attractive, but I sensed more than that. Something about the way she held herself—I knew she would be just as beautiful inside as she was outside. I knew she was the girl God wanted me to meet.

Of course, I couldn't help wondering how my cousin knew this girl. Were they friends or had she just shown up, the friend of a friend, perhaps? As I was thinking all of these questions she walked up to me and said, "Hi, I'm Emily."

"Hey, Emily. My name's Joe. I'm Patrick's cousin." I tried to sound smooth.

"Patrick has told me a lot about you," she said with a smile.

"Oh, cool! How'd you guys meet?" I asked, wondering what, exactly, Patrick had told her about me.

"We met at Spill the Beans, an ice-cream shop in downtown Clemson. Our friends are all in engineering classes together, and we hang out outside of classes."

"That's awesome. So, are you guys going out with us tonight?"

"Uh, yes!" She looked at me as if I were stupid. "I think we are."

At that moment, Patrick's friends walked into the room and we parted ways. Keeping to myself I noticed Emily and some guy apparently had something going on. Unbeknownst to The Citadel boys, she had already gone on a date with the guy, and rumor had it that they'd already kissed. This guy she was talking to had already beaten me to it. More girls walked in, friends of Emily or Patrick.

Caleb, Kyle, and I made eye contact across the room, giving each other the look that friends share, that look that says: *This is going to be a great night.* Caleb liked to call himself the land shark, because he had this persona about him that, no matter what, he could get any girl in the world. "The land shark's going to eat tonight," he said as he took a seat next to me on Patrick's futon. "No one is safe, especially if your girl has a boyfriend." Kyle and I laughed.

"Man, you are all talk, bro," Kyle said.

A couple more minutes passed before Kyle decided it was time to go to the fraternity party. My other cousin, John, a senior brother of Pi Kappa Alpha chapter at Clemson, was having a party at the Lambda Chi house. According to more than one source, the Citadel cadets are honorary members of Kappa Alpha. Robert E. Lee was that fraternity's spiritual founder, which means all cadets at military colleges in the South are honorary members. Couple that with my cousin being a senior at his own event and rolling in with seven beautiful girls, and nothing was going to stop this from being a night to remember!

One of Pat's friends volunteered to be the designated driver—a good ol' Southern Baptist boy who didn't like to drink. He had a super nice pickup truck that fit all of us, with the girls in the cab and the guys piled in the truck bed. It was a starry, moonless night. I couldn't help but think of how awesome it would be to be in that truck bed with Emily, lying face up, looking up at the stars, instead of packed in there with these drunk guys.

While I was daydreaming about such a nice date, Big Weaves, Kyle, announced that we had arrived. I turned my head and saw a two-story house out in the middle of nowhere with tons of cars parked in front. We had arrived at the Lambda Chi fraternity house.

This would be the first fraternity party any of us had ever attended. What if they wouldn't let us in? We considered this possibility before trying our luck. None of us were in a fraternity, nor had we brought any alcohol. But we did have a number of girls with us and my cousin was a senior brother, so there was that. Either way, they were going to have to let us in or else Kyle, Caleb and I were going to have to open a nice can of whoop-ass.

"Oh, you just cursed," Mary exclaimed.

"I'm sorry. I get a little carried away when describing my friends. Our mentality anywhere we go is that we are the 'baddest' mother you-know-what's in town."

We were still discussing how we could ensure that we'd be admitted to the party when I got the wise idea to ask the group for a girl's number in case we got separated from them. My friends looked at me with incredulity. This was a bold move on my part. I just hoped it would go as planned.

Good thing for us all, it did. It went exactly as planned. "I'll give you my number," Emily said.

That, my friends, is called high risk/high reward. I could have gotten any girl's number and the love story between me and Emily would have ended there; but by the grace of God and His divine intervention, it was Emily who offered first, giving me her number right there in front of everyone.

"Wow, I think Emily likes you!" someone said. Well, I sure hoped so.

It was time to head into the party. I was feeling like the man. I was at my first college fraternity party—at a premiere ACC school—with my best friends, and I had just gotten a number from the girl of my dreams (whom, by the way, I was about to party with for the next five hours). One could say that the stars were aligning. We walked into the house. Music was blowing the speakers off the walls. Lights were flashing everywhere. Except for a pool table, there was literally no other furniture in the house, though there was a fireplace in one wall. The rest of the house was filled with people, alcohol, and the special effects of music and lights.

It was like a scene from a movie. I was in awe. The music. The lights. All around us, girls were dancing and hooking up with guys. It was everything a young freshman in college would hope to experience at his first fraternity party. Kyle chimed in, "To think we're locked up at The Citadel, missing out on this experience every weekend, and even sometimes during the week." *Dang*, I thought. He was right. We *were* missing out on a lot of fun, but I was glad I chose to go to The Citadel anyway. There's no way I'd be able to prioritize partying *and* school work. Thank the Lord for blessing me with my decision.

Caleb, Kyle, and I stood out in the crowd like sore thumbs. Not only were we the only bald people at the party, but we were also the only eighteen- and nineteen-year-old kids who had not experienced college life yet, at least not at a normal non-military school.

My goal for the night was to get Emily to dance with me and maybe to have our first kiss. With nothing to lose, I approached her. "Do you want to dance?"

"No, thank you. I'm just going to hang here with my friends and talk." Meanwhile, I saw all of my friends dancing with other college girls. Caleb was on cloud nine, while I was in a state of confusion.

I hate mind games, and Emily had just opened an entire playbook called "playing hard to get." I brushed it off and with no worries went off with Pat and proceeded to enjoy the party. The music was loud and the people were going crazy.

The fraternity party was a great introduction to real college life for me. Though I had a great time, I was disappointed that I hadn't gotten my kiss—or even a dance—from the girl of my dreams. To make matters worse, summer was about to start, which meant she would be going back home to Maryland and I wouldn't be able to see her until the following fall semester on bye week or after we play Clemson. And to make matters even worse than that, my cousin's entire group of friends had started crushing over her.

I had her number, though, so we kept in touch. Not dating—just talking. The fact that every guy she hung out with wanted to date her bothered me a great deal. Oh well, what could I do? She was in Clemson and I was in Charleston, after all. I focused on my school work and went home for the month of May after finishing up knob year. It wasn't until I was packing my things to return to The Citadel for fall football camp when Patrick asked me in a text if I remembered that girl Emily from Clemson (Did I remember her? I laughed out loud. Really, he didn't know that we had kept in touch). Her family was moving to Atlanta, he said, and he wanted to help her move. I nearly jumped out of my seat. Crap, I hoped that my cousin didn't have feelings for her. I didn't want to let him know that she and I had been talking. To make matters worse, the day she moved to Atlanta was my last day home before I reported to fall football camp at The Citadel.

Months went by without me seeing her. Thinking that she was no longer interested in me, I accepted that it was best that we moved on. I mean, it was already tough that she was at Clemson and already had so many guys that liked her. Well, at least that's what I thought until one Tuesday afternoon in October. I was in my barracks room killing time until I had to report to meetings and later, practice. Chris was sleeping away the day because he only had two classes. (I swear, that kid never went to class.) Up in my bed I was doing some reading for my biology class. I was reading about genomes and other microbiology. It was quite interesting stuff. Did you know that we are the only living organism that knows it is made up of other living organisms? Very trippy. As I was enthralled with the text, my phone started to ring. I looked at the caller ID and answered, "Hello?"

"Hey, is this Joe?" My caller ID said it was Emily, but I wasn't sure if it really was her or not, so I decided to play along with it.

"Yes, it is. Who's this?"

"It's Emily." The moment she uttered those words, my heart started racing and I had butterflies in my stomach. What did she want? We hadn't talked in a long time, so I knew she had called for a reason.

"Well, I haven't heard from you in a while and I just wanted to see how you've been doing." There was no way she just wanted to talk and see how I had been without having something else for me. It turned out she had been thinking about me as much as I had been thinking about her. We caught up for twenty minutes before I had to leave for practice.

Caleb came by my room so we could walk to practice together.

"Caleb, guess what, man?"

"What?"

"You remember Emily from Clemson, right?"

He looked at me. "Emily from Clemson… nope."

"Remember Patrick and Hannah's friend?"

"Ah, Emily…. How's my girl doing?"

"She's good, man, but you're never going to believe this…. She just called me and we talked for almost half an hour."

He looked at me, unimpressed. "Good for you, man. She probably likes you." I just smiled as we walked into Seignious Hall. The thought of seeing her again excited me.

For the next couple of weeks, we continued to text and talk on the phone. After about a month, we started to Skype almost every other night. Months and months went by while we were talking, and it killed me not being able to physically leave campus to see her. To compound the agony, my second season was a long and losing one. It was the first losing season I had ever had in my thirteen-year football career. I hate losing. We had put in so much time and effort in the off season that it almost felt insulting to be on a team that could not produce. Looking back at that season, I'm still ashamed of the way we played. It was just a bunch of individuals on the field. We weren't a team. The following semester did not lessen in hardship. The pressure was at an all-time high that spring semester with workouts, spring ball, and classes. Also, I was competing for a starting position, and it was all getting to me. Thank the Lord for spring break.

For spring break, Kyle and I decided to vacation together. We drove down to Atlanta to fly with my dad and our family friends to go skiing in Breckinridge, Colorado. Most of my teammates were going on a cruise or partying in Florida. If you have not gone to Breckenridge, you're missing out. It's the most fun skiing destination in the country; well, that or Park City, Utah. The funny thing is, though… before we flew all the way out there to ski, Kyle started talking all this junk: "Dude, I'm an athlete and a great skier. I did double black diamonds out in West Virginia growing up." I smiled because a green out West is equivalent to a black on the East Coast.

"What's a black and a green?" the little girl asked me.

"Those are the difficulty levels of skiing. Green is usually for beginners and is not that hard of a run to ski down, while black is an expert level, which means it's quite challenging."

She smiled in amusement. "Oh, I see. Well, Mr. Joe, what are you?"

"I'm a blue skier. Not the best, but through practice I've gotten quite good. Let's just say… my man Kyle was in for a rude awakening."

When we got on peak six, Kyle fell completely off the gondola.

"Kyle, I thought you said you were good," my dad chided him.

"Mr. Crochet, I just have to warm up is all."

Well, we were out there for four days and he was still warming up on our last day. I don't think he ever went down a single run without wiping out.

The whole time I was in Colorado, I couldn't stop thinking about

Emily. I had to find a way to see her during spring break. Fortunately, we had time to make something happen. We flew back Friday. This gave us two more days of break. Kyle and I came up with a quick plan and decided to throw a party at my parents' lake house (unbeknownst to them). My brother and all his friends from high school drove up to the lake house to meet us. My cousin Patrick and his friends drove down from Clemson, along with some sorority girls he knew. Emily, Hannah, and Aurie—one of Emily's friends—drove down separately from Clemson as well. Sure, I was nervous about hosting a party and seeing Emily again, but most of all I was excited.

Kyle and I, along with some of my other friends from high school, headed to the lake house early to prepare for what was going to be a great night. A couple of hours passed before people started to show up. Our Facebook invitation had stipulated that this event was BYOA – bring your own alcohol. Of course, at our age that would be hard to do without a fake ID. I was not about to commit an HV over getting some alcohol.

"Mr. Joe, what's an HV?" Mary asked.

"An honor violation. The Citadel is built on three pillars: honor, duty, and respect. Violating the honor code can get you a one-way ticket to getting kicked out of school."

So, back to the party. It started at sundown. Games such as beer pong and flip cup were the main event. Patrick and I had been running the table all night. There was not a team or a pair of individuals in the house that could beat us. Kyle and my brother were probably the only two guys that it would come down to the last cup. The music was loud and everyone seemed to be having a good time... well, everyone except for Emily. I totally forgot to even talk to her. I knew she was here. Heck, she was the only reason why I decided to throw the party in the first place. Suddenly, my shots were not going into the cups. My mojo was down. If you really think about it, beer pong is such a mindless game. You stand there and throw a ping pong ball into a red solo cup for hours. It was time to refocus and rearrange my priorities.

After losing to my brother and Kyle, I bolted upstairs to check on Emily and her friends. I said, "I am so sorry for not being able to properly host you guys." I looked right into Emily's eyes.

Aurie chimed in, "Well, damn, Joe--you better be. I mean, we've been sitting up here all by ourselves."

I turned to Emily. "Can I show you something cool?" She nodded and smiled, so I grabbed her hand. "Follow me. I'm sure it's something you've never seen before."

"Where are we going?" she asked, still holding my hand.

"Almost there." I didn't want to ruin the surprise.

The pathway to the dock was under a ton of pine and oak tree branches that blocked the view of the stars. Thank the Lord for walkway lights, or else we would not have been able to get there. The songs of crickets and frogs filled the air, interrupted by the occasional smack of a beaver tail upon the water.

Emily had never been on a dock before. Well, not like this one, at least. This dock was in a private cove overlooking the south end of Lake Oconee. At night, it's one of the most beautiful sights to see.

When we moved from beneath the canopy of trees, the night sky with its millions of stars unfurled above us. We took our first steps on the dock, and she was speechless at first. "Joseph, this is so beautiful," she finally whispered. It was a crystal-clear night. There were more stars in the sky than the blackness in outer space. A shooting star appeared almost every thirty seconds and the moon was just starting to rise. We sat down on my father's thirty-year-old bench that he and his brother Bubba made when they first purchased the property back in 1984.

We sat looking up at the sky for hours, but it felt like only seconds had passed. It is really true that time stands still when you're with the girl you love. All the worries in the world disappeared and my sole focus was on her. I recalled some words of advice about love: *You know when you know.* I knew she was the one from the moment I set eyes on her, and I could feel it more than ever that night. I needed to at least tell her how I felt. This could be my one and only shot, and like I said earlier, life begins the moment you take that first step outside of your comfort zone.

I looked Emily in the eyes. "Emily, I'm really glad you came tonight. I've been wanting to tell you this for a while now. I like you a lot and would love it if I could kiss you."

She smiled so stunningly at me. The moonlight shone off her face and made her smile glisten in the night. Without saying anything, she turned her head at me and I turned mine to hers and we kissed. Sparks flew like fireworks on the Fourth of July. It was an amazing first kiss and the start of something much more than puppy love.

"There is nothing permanent except change."

- HERACLITUS

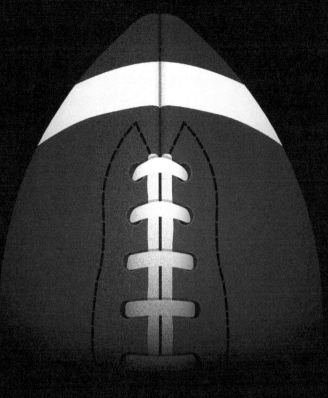

YEAR THREE

Red-Shirt

Sophomore Season

Chapter 4:

THE TURN OF THE TIDE IN CHARLESTON, SC

Charleston is such a beautiful place. I walked out on the Battery, looking at the Charleston Harbor and saw the richness of history. There is not a better place in the world to watch a sunset or a sunrise. As I looked out at the Charleston Harbor, I saw the beautiful Ravenel Bridge scraping the sky. It is a pillar bridging the Charleston peninsula and Mount Pleasant. The architectural design is something that Leonardo da Vinci or Michelangelo could not have envisioned, a true masterpiece that towers over this great city skyline. I looked out into the water to keep an eye on my fishing line. The Battery is known for good fishing during the summertime, when the waves are not as crazy. I used cut mullet on a Carolina rig to bottom fish. I just wanted to catch something. I was with Kyle, Eric, and Caleb. These three guys, though lousy fishermen, helped keep my cool even at the hottest times, whether it be at The Citadel or in the summer heat in Charleston. They were my voice of reason in such a high-stress environment. It went without saying that I would do anything in the world for them, and I know in return they would do the same for me as well. It was about 4:00 in the afternoon, hot and humid. We hadn't even gotten one bite.

Though we were fishing, we were also soaking in the beauty of a summer day in the greatest city in the world. Times like this were truly great for appreciating God's masterpiece. The seagulls and pelicans were flying high above us, the palmetto palms were blowing in the cool Charleston breeze, and we heard kids playing in the park in the distance. These things were going on simultaneously while I was hanging out with my "dogs." What a great time to be alive! A couple of hours went by as we sat and watched our poles. Then the tide changed and started going out to sea. This was our cue to stop fishing, because as soon as the tide starts going out it's almost impossible to catch anything. As we were reeling in our rods, *Wham!*—my rod got hit. A fish had bitten my bait! The guys sat and watched as I reeled the bad boy in, yelling, "Caleb, grab the net."

"Dang, Joe—you seem to be struggling pulling that bad boy in," Kyle said.

"Well, guys, it doesn't feel like much, but it hit my pole as if it were a decent-sized fish," I shot back at him, all the while hoping to God there would be something alive on the other end. Watch there not be anything at all. Watch it be an old tire or piece of junk. That would be the whipped cream and cherry on top of my fishing stories. I kept reeling until the ugliest fish I'd ever seen appeared, gasping for water. Caleb and Kyle burst out laughing. "Dude, are you sure that's even a fish?" Eric queried.

What I had caught was a dog-head fish.

I had it out of the water for maybe ten seconds when a local came over, took his knife from his pocket, stabbed the fish in the head, and threw it back into the water. "That fish no good," he exclaimed, wiping his hand on his pants as he went back to his own rod and reel.

"Caleb, your wife is going to look like a dog-head fish one day," I said to my friend.

"No, Joe. That'll be what your daughter looks like," he fired back.

I fired back at him and we went back and forth like this for a couple minutes, laughing and having fun while Eric and Kyle looked on, shaking their heads.

"Lighten up a little, guys. We're just joking," I told them.

"Yeah, take a chill pill," Caleb chimed in.

Those were the best of times.

Fishing was a new hobby for us. I'd been learning about the tides and how the tide affects the fish you might catch. For instance, I had learned from the Weather Channel that the tide changes every thirteen hours. In this area it receded until the harbor resembled a marsh, and then flowed back with a force to fill the harbor six feet deep. I had learned that the moon had something to do with the tides, pulling them in and pushing them out in some way.

We fished a lot the rest of that summer. At Breech Inlet we caught whiting, baby black tip sharks, redfish, and bluefish. The more we fished, the better we got at it, and that made us want to do it even more. Fall semester flew by with our new-found hobby. We fished on the weekends when we didn't have football; we fished during the week after classes, and even during our break periods on final exam days.

I had just finished my last exam for the fall semester and I was ready to head home for holiday break. Before departing, I drove out the dock with Caleb to watch the tide come in. I remember sitting out there on that dock, reflecting on the past season with my friend and teammate. Our season last year was terrible. It was embarrassing to have to live with our 5-7 record (4-4 SoCon). No doubt about it: We sucked. I had never been on a losing team in my life. Something needed to change.

It was tough, because we knew that that record would be our identity until we could prove our worth the next season.

Not only was our record dismal, but the culture of the program was also at an all-time low. It lacked a lot of things, but most importantly it lacked leadership. The coaching staff didn't get along. Coaches were angry about other coaches having a higher title, and their resentment affected the team. In the locker room, nobody cared except our class about what was best for the team. It was just a room filled with individuals. Caleb and I were so frustrated, because we lost a lot of games we should have won, and all we could do as non-starters and non-captains was talk about the changes we would make come our time. The team needed a culture shock. I just didn't know how we were going to do it. We had the talent to be a championship team. We just needed to get all the guys on board with seeing the vision and believing it. Little did I know that God was listening to our entire conversation the entire time.

After talking with Caleb, I felt hopeless about the future of our program. It had been a grueling fall semester—not just having a losing season but losing big time to Clemson. Honestly, I didn't even know if I wanted to continue my career at The Citadel; however, I quickly snapped out of that mindset. I had to put it in the past in order to pursue my goal, which was to be the best student-athlete that I could be. The first step of that—and my goal for the upcoming semester—was to be a starter and to do everything in my power to get faster, stronger, and better.

I looked at Caleb. "Alright man, I better head out if I'm going to make it back to Georgia at a decent hour."

Caleb still had two exams left to take. "Leaving so soon?" he asked as we rose to our feet. "Well, enjoy your break, Joe. Have a safe drive, and God bless."

"God bless, Brother!" I said as we hugged it out.

I hopped into my 2006 4Runner, turned the key, and drove away with some Brantley Gilbert on the stereo. An hour or so later, my phone started going off.

"Caleb—what's up?" I said after accepting the call.

"Hello... Joe?"

"What's up, man?" I said with a bit of panic, thinking something drastic must have happened. I mean I had just seen Caleb and everything was fine.

"Have you heard the news?"

"News... what news?"

"The news about Coach Higgins?"

"No what happened?" All sorts of scenarios ran through my brain in that instant. Death, accidents, injuries, firings.

"Bro... he's leaving. He accepted a coaching job at Wake Forest."

"What... Coach Higgins is leaving...? What does that mean for us or the other coaching staff?"

This was not something I had seen coming. While I was being recruited back in high school, Antonio Goss, position coach of Furman, warned me that a coaching change during my time might happen. Dang, I had really liked getting to know Coach Higgins. He was a wise coach who knew a lot about the game.

"Dude, I don't know. I just know that he called all the remaining players that had not left for Christmas break into the meeting room to tell us."

"So, it looks like we don't have a coach," I said.

"Yeah, Joe, we're coach-less and nobody knows what's going to happen," Caleb said in a sarcastic tone, though I guess there was truth to his words. For the moment, at least.

Over break, even more news came out. They were really cleaning house. The Citadel was hiring a new head coach, a new athletic director, and a new media relations director. As far as I knew, Andy (the head athletic director) and his medical staff, and Coach Donnell and his strength and conditioning staff were the only ones remaining. All during my break, I didn't know who the new coach would be. Another concern of mine was whether or not the new coach (whoever he might be) would even honor my football scholarship. Would I have to transfer? The uncertainty really put a damper on my holiday break.

We reported back in early January. At our first team meeting, we learned that Coach Houston, former head coach of Lenoir Rhyne, had been hired as the new head coach of The Citadel Bulldogs. January 9th was to be his first day.

Pessimism and uncertainty filled the locker room ahead of his arrival. *Coach Houston—who is he? A Division II coach is our new head coach?* Our program needed change; however, as humans we tend to fear and resist change.

Coach Donnell, Coach D, came into the locker room to quell our unease. "As assistant athletic director, I've had the privilege of meeting Coach Houston. Y'all are going to meet him tomorrow and you'd better bring your A-game to conditioning. He's not the kind of guy that'll put up with a 5-7 program."

And boy, was Coach D right. I knew from the moment I first laid eyes on Coach Houston that things would be different. He was a very intimidating guy. His chest looked like it could bench press five hundred pounds, and he had a fire behind him that was lit and not going to burn out anytime soon. "If you guys think being 5-7 is ok, well then by golly you'd better leave, because this game is not for you," he yelled at us as we were bear crawling and doing things that gave us pain in certain areas for days. Looking at my teammates after the morning workout, I could tell that we were all feeling it. We bitched and moaned for the rest of the day.

Coach Houston immediately set to work making changes in the former coaching staff. He let go of everyone except for Coach Gunter, who at the time oversaw recruiting. Apparently, Coach Gunter had also been a graduate assistant for Coach Houston at Lenoir Rhyne. (Life lesson, Mary: It's not *what* you know but *who* you know in life). Coach Houston and his new coaching staff brought with them a new culture, a new energy, and the mindset that we were a championship program. The tide had finally turned in Charleston, South Carolina and it would be bringing us to a great destination.

Coach Tripp Weaver, former spring game quarterback for East Carolina University, was going to be my new position coach. Coach Maurice Drayton, former defensive backs coach at Coastal Carolina, was going to be the defensive coordinator. This would be the second defensive coordinator I had had since I started in 2012. My freshman year, Coach Aashon Larkins was my position coach. The next year, I moved to the hybrid outside linebacker-defensive end position under Coach Denny Doornbos. I enjoyed being in Coach Doornbos's room with Bay Amrhein, Derek Douglas, Mark Thomas, and Mitchell Jeter. It was a more relaxed atmosphere, and we could strictly focus on strategy.

I was in for a surprise when I met my new position coach. I walked to his office expecting to meet a fiery, hard-nosed jacked mother you-know-what, but when I stepped inside his office, I was greeted by a guy who seemed to be about twenty-five years old. He didn't look like a college athlete, especially not like a football player.

"Hey, do you know where Coach Weaver is?" I said.

"Yeah, he's right here," he replied, smiling. I was taken back.

"Coach Weaver...?"

"Yep, That's me. What's your name?"

"I'm Joe Crochet."

"Ah, Joe—what's going on?" He motioned for me to take a seat across from him and we chatted for several minutes about the team and the game. Immediately I could tell that he knew what he was talking about. The terminology he used and the manner with which he carried himself were very serious.

But having a new coach meant more than just adjusting to a new team culture and personality. It also meant trying out for my position on the team once again. And of course, there was the issue of my scholarship. Once I felt comfortable with him, I couldn't help but blurt it out.

"Hey, Coach, what's the deal about my scholarship? I'm planning on graduating early to pursue my master's. Will y'all still honor that?"

He looked at me regretfully. "Joe, we're going to honor your scholarship, but as soon as you graduate, we're not going to be able to pay for your fifth year."

My blood started to boil. "Really? Well, that's a shame because Kate Brown, my academic advisor, and I had devised a plan from the very beginning planning out my schedule for me to graduate in three and a half years specifically so I could knock out my MBA the following spring and fall semester during my last year of eligibility."

As I was saying this, it occurred to me that FCS schools are limited to offering sixty-five full scholarships each year. They had not seen me play or practice but were basing this decision on my tangibles, such as game stats from the previous year and weight room numbers. The only way I was going to be able to change their minds was by showing up every day and giving one hundred and ten percent effort to earn my position. I had to show them how much of an asset I was to the team. I had to show them they needed me come the beginning of my red-shirt senior year. I left the meeting fired up, ready to prove to them and to myself that I could be a great football player for the team and the program.

I remember writing out my goals for the following season. Academically, I wanted to push the limits and complete my four-year degree in three years. I wanted to graduate with honors and then complete my MBA in three semesters. Athletically, by next season I needed to be a starter, and by the following season an All-Conference player, and then my last season I needed to be an All-American. I had drawn up the vision. I was on board with the new coaching staff. We were either going to make it to the promised land or going to sink on the way there. Either way, the ship was leaving, and I made sure to find a seat.

The following season we opened against Florida State. They had just won the FBS National Championship the year before and James Winston was returning for his final season after winning the Heisman Trophy. They were ranked number one in the country during the preseason and we were their home opener. It's no surprise that we didn't win, but we played really well, especially considering the mismatch in our teams.

"You come against me with sword and spear and javelin, but I come against you in the name of the Lord Almighty, the God of the armies of Israel, whom you have defied."

\- DAVID, THE BIBLE

Chapter 5:

THE CITADEL FELLOWSHIP OF CHRISTIAN ATHLETES

Faith has a way of bringing out the best in people during the toughest times. In my life, it has always been the cornerstone upon which I base my morals and values. In times of darkness, it takes faith to push us through. The famous saying, *There are no atheists in a foxhole* applies more often than not during turbulent waters. For example, there are countless tales of non-believers fighting in World War II who converted to Christianity on the day of battle simply because the religion was a crutch to heal and calm them.

God did not put us on Earth to live a life of fear. The great S. Truett Cathy once said, "Do your best and let God do the rest." After reading his book *How Did You Do It, Truett?* inspiration flooded my mind. I'm a dreamer, always have been, but this book helped me see the art of pursuing my dreams and one day making them into a reality. All it takes is hard work, a little luck, and dedication to believe in following your dreams. You are reading this book, but before this got put down on paper, it was only a dream.

Pushing yourself to live outside your comfort zone is not easy; many avoid or resist it. For me, knowing that God is putting me on his path, a path that He specifically designed for me, delivers courage and easement. My understanding about religion and God has kept me strong through many years of hardship. I know you are probably thinking that a healthy middle-class white boy from Atlanta, GA has not had any true experience of hardship. Well, let me tell you, I have. I suffer from a posttraumatic stress disorder, anxiety disorder, and depression. You never know what type of inner battle someone is experiencing. They may look like strong, tough football players on the outside, while inside they are struggling emotionally or on the verge of collapse. People put on all kinds of facades to hide their inner turmoil. That's why it's important never to judge a book by its cover. Until you walk in someone else's footsteps, you have no grounds to cast judgment.

Anyway, where was I, oh yes…The Citadel was not an easy school to attend, let alone play a sport at. Fortunately, a man named RaShan Frost could implement the gospel in times when I needed the Lord the most. His nickname to all the players was Frosty. I called him Coach Frost. Coach Frost was a former SEC Division I football player. He played defensive line for the Auburn Tigers from 1996 to 1999. At The Citadel, Coach Frost was the campus director for the Fellowship of Christian Athletes, more commonly known as FCA. He also served as the chaplain and character coach for the team, a role that he had been in since 2013. Frosty was the man!

The first day I met Frosty was at a Citadel FCA meeting. Every Monday during lunchtime the FCA meets. To some it was a social gathering and a valid excuse for getting out of going to formation and having to do push-ups. To others, it was a form of church because they were not able to hear the word on Sunday due to being too busy or simply just hung over from the night before. For me, it was a time that

I could really dig deeper into my faith with Christ.

Frosty had this ability to speak candidly and passionately about the Gospel and to relate it to our lives. His fire and ability to formulate a relatable message to such a diverse and young audience was a gift. Growing up, I always feared public speaking. I hated being at the center of attention and having other people staring at me. The mere thought of it gave me anxiety. One thing I admired about Frosty was his ability to stand up confidently in front of others and not budge, to reach out to people with open arms instead of shutting them out with closed fists.

"Wow, Frosty seems like an open guy," Mary said. "He reminds me of my camp counselor back at summer camp. All he does is preach the Gospel and make us feel good about being followers of Christ."

"Wow, your friend seems like an awesome guy. He sounds very similar to Frosty."

"Yeah," she agreed. "He's the best!"

During my freshman year, I went to FCA meetings every Monday. It was a great time to reflect on life, count my blessings, and socialize with my fellow teammates. It helped me tremendously during knob year because it gave me something to look forward to. Sunday nights I could have dreaded what the week would bring: sweep detail, formation, being bald and locked inside a large confined facility. Or, I could look forward to going to FCA every Monday morning. When I woke up, I knew all I had to do was make it a couple of hours and then it would be FCA time.

During the season, every Thursday after practice and dinner Frosty and guys from the team got together in Seignious Hall for Bible study. Known as Fight Club, it was a time to have fellowship and worship the Lord. Frosty would sit in a revolving computer chair at the front of the room while all the rest of us scattered around the room. He started off by asking one of us to lead the opening prayer. Usually Rashad, Dondray, Vinny, or DaSean took the initiative. I was more of a quiet guy in group settings and just liked to reflect on all the blessings God had given me so far. Following the opening prayer, Frosty would say, "It's time to get this medicine," and recite Philippians 4:13, "I can do all things through Christ who gives me strength," and read a passage from the Bible. After he read the passage, we would have a group discussion, debating and discussing for almost thirty minutes. His ability to relate the scripture to our lives was a testament of his gift and talent to motivate us through the word.

Though I was raised Catholic, my parents would send me to Smoke Rise Baptist Summer Camp every year. It was there that I truly learned about God. A guy named Gregg led Bible study there in a way that was very similar to how Frosty did it—with a smooth transition from the words in the Bible to some aspect of our own lives. Gregg described the Bible as a weapon against Satan. Frosty called it the spiritual sword. I truly believe in good and evil. Most importantly, I believe that the power of prayer can work miracles. Prayer has helped me during my toughest times. It was a cornerstone for me during knob year and whenever I lost a loved one. It has always given me strength, because I know God has a plan for me, that He's taking me along on this journey for a reason. I believe everything happens for a reason.

Anyway, back to the story. There were also FCA meetings on Mondays at lunchtime, and these meetings were open to all sports programs and even to normal cadets just looking to get away from the madness and gather around to hear the Word. Frosty usually provided pizza, sending me and Kyle to pick up thirty pizzas from the canteen. The trick was monitoring some of the offensive linemen on how many slices they would get. There was only enough for two slices per person, and trust me, those guys can eat.

The best blessing about Frosty was on game day. As a former football player, SEC Defensive tackle, he could relate to the pre-game feelings and rituals. Ever since he became our team chaplain, he made it a point to do something special on game days such as arranging for a guest speaker to preach the word or delivering the message himself. Either way, the Word kept us spiritually strong. It was the fire needed to strengthen our iron!

If you question the existence of God or anything in that realm, I will just give you one example that will change your entire thought process on the subject: Imagine the world as a huge library made up of billions of books. Each book in the world library represents a human being. There are billions of books that have been written throughout time all around the world. Every book is different, made up of different words, sentences, and paragraphs that come together creating a different narrative. If I ask, "Can a book create itself?" you would think that's silly, right? There is no way a book can just appear out of the blue. It took an intelligent being, such as a human, to take the time to gather his thoughts, to develop intelligent words to form sentences, to piece paragraphs into chapters and ultimately create a book.

Our DNA is our book. Over the billions of years of our universe's existence, it did not just happen through evolution that our binary code created itself; rather, it took an intelligent being, God, to develop and write our code, just like an author writes a book. This book you are reading was created by me. It took my intellectual well-being to create this manuscript. All of this did not happen because of chance. If that were the case, then words would just form together and a book would be able to write itself. We did not just randomly come into the world. We were created by God. I am a Christian, but I am not telling you what to believe in. I'm just challenging you to step out of your comfort zone and ask the hard questions. I promise you that doing so will point to there being a higher, more intelligent power: God.

Anyway, back to the story. Where was I…oh yes, Coach Frosty! On Game days, we arrived at the stadium two hours before kickoff. We gathered as a team on the fifty-yard line in a prayer circle. We linked arms and listened to Frosty bless the field and the team. "God protect these young men, players, dogs, as they go out to play today. Lord, I ask that you keep them safe and allow them to play with relentless effort. I ask that you give them the strength and ability to play the game for your glory. In Jesus' name, Amen."

At the end of the day, it's all about giving back to God for the talents He has given us. Every day we wake up it is a miracle, and I try to be the best person I can be every day and have a positive influence on each and every person's life.

The FCA meant a lot to our team and to this great institution. I swear one day when I have the money, I'm going to give back to Frosty and The Citadel FCA. It's an under-budgeted program that does so much; however, it is limited to a budget given by the State. Many times, Frosty put up his own money to pay for the food that we ate on Mondays.

Many influential people in FCA made a tremendous impact on my relationship with God. Guys like Keith, Rashad, Frosty, Kyle, Dondray, Caleb, and Eric have actively challenged me in my faith and kept me on a straight path. Their positive attitudes were inspiring. Having teammates strong in faith played a huge role in my beliefs. Several times I struggled with my faith and had my doubts; however, each time I was at my lowest, someone picked me back up and showed me it was going to be okay. "It's all God, so it's all good" was something we said in the locker room. It's all about perspective: if I kept God in the centermost part of my life, He would not lead me down a broken path that I couldn't handle.

Every year, Frosty scheduled a retreat for FCA members. Usually he scheduled it on an inspection weekend so that not only were members able to get away and worship God, but the added bonus of missing an SMI might tempt them to want to praise the Lord a little more.

"What are SMIs?" Mary asked.

"Saturday morning inspection. They lasted from 5:45 AM till around noon. The TAC officers, retired or inactive duty military officers, inspected every cadet's uniform and room during that time. If you so much as had a speck of dust on your half press, you were going to get marked for it. I have not met one cadet that likes SMI's. Actually… that's false, there was this upperclassman, a grade older than me, that loved everything about it. He was the cadet that loved checking for all-ins, too. In fact, he got me in trouble on the one night I ever went AWOL, but that's a different story."

"AWOL, what's that?"

"AWOL means absent without leave. It's when you leave campus when you're not supposed to. I only did it once, and unfortunately, I got caught. Promise me you won't go AWOL if you ever go to The Citadel, Mary.

"Every year, Frosty scheduled a retreat for FCA members. Fortunately, during knob year Frosty scheduled a retreat on Kiawah Island at a place called Camp St. Christopher, and I was granted a leave of absence from that inspection day."

"Is leave of absence the same thing as AWOL?"

"No, a leave of absence is different from AWOL, because my leave was approved by the proper chain of command. Going AWOL means leaving without permission."

"Ah, okay, I think I got it now!"

Camp St. Christopher was awesome. We weren't the only FCA group there. There were FCAs from other colleges such as NC State,

Virginia Tech, Charleston Southern and the College of Charleston. We played games, worshipped the Lord, and did community service together. The camp was right on the beach, too. The water was completely still and peaceful, without a wave in sight. One night we gathered around the campfire, singing songs and getting to know the people from different schools. It truly was a great place to get away from the world and lift in prayer. I much rather would have been there than in the barracks preparing for an SMI. Those were some of the greatest moments I have had worshipping the Lord.

However, when there are highs there must also be lows. It doesn't hit you until something tragic happens and makes you think how truly blessed you are. During the second week of spring practice, DaSean, our starting fullback, collapsed at practice. I was on the defense going against him. Before he fell, he had just completed a huge run. He was killing our defense. He was a great player. In fact, his performance in spring ball had highlighted him as our best fullback and likely starter for the fall season.

DaSean was from the same area as me. He had studied at Greater Atlanta Christian Academy and trained with many of my former teammates who went to Tucker High School. DaSean was one of the toughest people I knew. He had survived Ewing's sarcoma, a bone cancer. After numerous rounds of chemotherapy to treat a tumor on one of his left ribs, he was cleared to play football again. The Naval Academy wouldn't accept him after the cancer diagnosis, and that's how he came to The Citadel. It's all God's plan. Everything happens for a reason.

Of course, the practice stopped when he collapsed. Andy, our athletic trainer, tried to wake DaSean up, to no avail. The ambulance arrived in five minutes and the emergency responders picked him up, still in his shoulder pads, put him on a stretcher, and started wheeling him to the ambulance. What was going on? None of us knew what to do. I just wanted to run and make sure that he still had a pulse and was breathing. We said a prayer asking the Lord to be with DaSean and to watch over him, to give him strength to get through this.

Coach Houston called practice immediately. We showered up. Caleb and I left to go see if he was okay in the hospital. We arrived at the emergency room around 7:00 p.m. Coach Drayton and Coach Houston were there waiting outside while he was in surgery. Nobody knew if he was going to be all right; however, I had faith. In times like this, that is all one can do. I knew for a fact that DaSean was the strongest guy I had ever met. God couldn't just end the plan here. DaSean had to make it. All we could do was pray. We stayed at the hospital for about an hour, and then Coach told us that we should go back to campus. He said he would update us in the morning. DaSean's family was already on their way to Charleston. It was a moment like this that made me really appreciate my friends and family. This incident could happen to anyone at any time. I called my parents, my brother, and Emily and told them how much I loved them and cared about them. I could not sleep that night. I just kept looking at the ceiling in my top bunk, praying that he was going to be okay.

"Was he all right?" Mary asked, sadness in her eyes.

"Yes." I smiled at her. "Luckily, prayer works!"

According to the doctors, DaSean had suffered a brain aneurysm, and that's why he fell unconscious on the field. The emergency doctors were able to lower the swelling in his head. They said it was a miracle that he would be able to recover completely. Thank the Lord! He was going to be all right. Between surviving this as well as cancer… this guy is my hero—truly a walking miracle.

With all the great news, it seemed almost too good to be true. Sadly, it was. Though DaSean was going to be healed, he never would be able to play football again.

Coach Drayton preached about it all the time. "You never know when it will be your last play." It put life into perspective. All the stuff people complain about daily is minimal compared to the big picture. DaSean had shown me how awesome our Lord is. The fact that he survived two tough battles left no doubt in my mind that he was a testament to the fact that God has a plan for all of us. DaSean's ability to stay positive and see the world with a positive outlook even through those dark times was a true representation of Jesus working through him to shine light onto others. He is a living miracle, and I am so thankful to be his teammate and know him as a brother. Football is much more than just a game. It has brought me close to a lot of God-fearing individuals who challenge me to be the best person I can be.

"Wow, that is a miracle," Mary's mother chimed in.

"Well, being able to talk with you and Mary right now while sitting in a plane is a miracle. Every day you are awake, breathing, and living is a miracle. Don't ever forget that."

"I won't," said Mary. "Hey, Mommy? I have to go to the restroom."

"Okay, sweetheart, let's go," Mary's mom said, getting to her feet.

"Hey, Mister Joe, don't forget to tell me how you got that ring"

"I'll tell you when you return," I promised, and turned to look out the window at the clouds.

"There are no secrets to success. It is the result of preparation, hard work, and learning from failure."

\- COLIN POWELL

Chapter 6:

THE DAWG POUND

The weight room in Seignious Hall is known as the Dawg Pound, and it's no place for horsing around. You either bring in with you one hundred and ten percent of your effort and the willingness to be coachable, or you're not going to make it. It's where all the athletes from every sport go to train. A lot of people have come through the Dawg Pound but have not been able to achieve success because of their improper mindsets. Success does not just happen one day. It takes a lot of work, effort, proper training and time.

One definition of luck is that luck is the moment when preparation meets opportunity. It's that simple. Many people become "lucky" because they were prepared for the opportunity the moment it presented itself. Consider successful musicians as an example. They didn't just one day wake up and start singing and playing instruments and making money from doing so. Rather, they perfected their craft and when the opportunity presented itself—when the right person heard them, the manager of a recording label, for example—they were able to capitalize on it. Many people say practice makes perfect. That's a bunch of baloney. Of course, you must practice—again and again and again—but it's also essential that you practice in the right way. If you practice poorly, you will perform poorly. That's why you need a good coach. Effective coaches make sure you're practicing the right way. Only effective training and preparation build champions.

I think Coach Donnell Boucher is the best strength and conditioning coach on this planet. His formula of high-intensity training and his ability to organize workout plans are good, but his strongest asset is his ability to motivate players the moment they step into the weight room or onto the field. Any strength coach can help you improve in speed and strength, but Coach D has the ability to go beyond the obvious, to dive inside players' characters, molding them into wholesome men. The problem with other (less effective) training programs is that they don't develop players into men. They simply take boys and turn them into something freakishly athletic.

Coach D's training went beyond the field and beyond the sport. He counseled us on how to handle ourselves in public (as representatives of The Citadel). He helped us set weight and strength goals, taught us to discipline our images on social media, and a variety of other life lessons to help us make smarter decisions for our future.

Now, Coach D could get sentimental, and that was always kind of funny because he had a distinctive and unexpected voice—very deep and raspy. I remember stretching in the yoga room with soothing music playing in the background, a stark juxtaposition to Coach D's intensely male voice. Sometimes we couldn't help but laugh.

One of Coach D's talks was particularly memorable to me. It was when he told us the iceberg metaphor (which might actually be something Freud came up with). He drew a diagram of an iceberg on the board and we all looked around like he was nuts. "What's he gonna do? Talk about penguins?" one of the guy chortled from the back.

"All right guys, settle down," he said in his deep voice. "This diagram

I drew here is an iceberg. The iceberg is like anything in life. The tip of the iceberg represents success. It's the only visible part of the iceberg in the water. Just like most people on boats or swimming only see the tip of the iceberg, most people in life only see people as successful or not. They see the success you have as an individual, but what they don't know is that the tip of the iceberg is only ten percent of the entire ice structure. The part that people don't see are the countless hours of hard work in the weight room, on the field, in the classroom, the personal adversity that you have faced throughout your life, the troubles and the hard times. That's the ninety percent of what has brought you to this point. Nobody sees that." Damn, Coach hit us with some deep stuff.

This speech had me thinking all night, because he was totally right. The tendency nowadays is to judge a book by its cover without even reading the first page. We live in a society that is quick to judge and stereotype based on first impressions. All people are sinners, so why are we so quick to cast the first stone?

I found this talk extremely motivating. I reflected back on the times when I had felt dejected and rejected. I remembered when coaches from bigger schools had rejected me, basing their decision on the fact that—at age sixteen—I wasn't big enough. Furthermore, non-athlete peers had scoffed at my athletic ability, reminding me that I was only a player on a small-time football team and not some big shot SEC player. Those critics didn't know me personally. They knew nothing about the inner me or my inner drive and motivation. They were seeing only the tip of the iceberg.

When you're in the boxing ring, you can't focus on anything other than what is going on inside that ring. The same goes for life. There are so many distractions. Every day, people try to bash you and destroy you. This is why we loved Coach D—because he helped us understand that. He focused on building players, physically and mentally. Coaching was more than just a nine-to-five job for him: it was a passion.

"Mr. Joe, what's your tip of the iceberg?"

I looked down at Mary and told her that my tip of the iceberg was having a job for a Fortune 250 company, being a scholarship athlete playing a Division I sport, graduating with magna cum laude honors in three years, getting my MBA in a year in a half, being a starter for two conference championship teams, named first team All-SoCon player, and being a two time All-American; however, people don't see the number of hours, or the blood, sweat, and tears that went into that. "Wow, you did all that?" she said.

I did do all that—but I didn't do it alone. Many people helped me along the way. The problem with some people nowadays is that the tip of the iceberg is all they see. Who are they to critique me—or anyone, for that matter? While the average college students were partying, I was studying. While they were sleeping, I was working out. While they were tailgating on Saturdays, I was playing. Life is all about choices, and Coach D did a great job giving us a template for how to be success-ful in life. Every single person on our team had a tip of the iceberg, but also had ninety percent more of their life to offer as well. I challenge you to start viewing life in that same way and stop seeing just the tip.

At The Citadel, I played under four different position coaches. I enjoyed my time with each and every one; however, Coach Tripp Weaver was one of my all-time favorites. He was relatable, open, and honest with us. We could say anything around him. He was more of an older brother to me than a coach. He was open to us about his child-hood. He helped all of us understand what our "why" was and the real purpose for playing the game. For me, my "why" was that I was blessed with athletic ability and physique and that I was given the opportunity to learn from my mentors and play for something much greater than myself. "B.A.B" - Be a Baller, he used to say to us. "We all we got," he would say and we would reply: "We all we need." There was a culture of family within Seignious Hall, something that had not existed there since the early 1990s.

Summertime in the Dawg Pound was gruesome. We worked out every morning with conditioning, weight lifting, and speed and agility training. Tuesdays and Thursdays were the most difficult, because we also had to do position-specific drills as well as seven on seven. Each training session was harder than the previous one. Coach D had a method that tore you down but allowed you enough recovery time so you could come back and rebuild your muscles the next day. The only days we had off were right after the season ended during winter furlough, and a short while during the month of May to go home before returning for summer workouts. Most cadets and other people aren't aware of the time commitment football players make. During the season, football was like a full-time job on top of our classes and military obligations. We practiced Sunday, Tuesday, Wednesday, Thursday, traveled, went through game routine on Friday, and played the game on Saturday. We were required to be in Charleston eleven months a year and constantly sacrificed social time with family and friends for the sole purpose of being part of something bigger than ourselves.

My hope is to enlighten readers so they will have more respect for student-athletes, especially those at the highly disciplined Citadel. I know that there's a stereotype about student-athletes. Many view us as non-academic: they think we're not bright, that we've only been recruited for our brawn and agility and not for our intellect. But the truth is, we're all individuals. There might be some student athletes who don't take academics seriously (thereby perpetuating the stereotype), but there are others, like me, who are serious about academics and about football. The truth is that there are some of us who are academics first and athletes second. You shouldn't just look at an athlete and say to yourself, "Oh, he's an athlete, so he must not be a good student." We are not all the same, and for those athletes who are serious about academics, the struggle is real. Just think about how much easier my life would have been if I had only had to focus on school work and not on football.

"Teamwork is what the Green Bay Packers were all about. They didn't do it for individual glory. They did it because they loved one another."

- VINCE LOMBARDI

Chapter 7:

LEADERSHIP IN
THE DOG HOUSE

O rganizational leadership is the process of influencing people by providing purpose, direction, and motivation to accomplish a mission. Any team or organization is only as good as its leadership. An effective leader improves an organization by engendering the right values in its members. The Army has seven core values: loyalty, duty, respect, selfless service, honor, integrity, and personal courage. But these values extend well beyond the military—leaders of any great organization must possess and exude these qualities. At The Citadel, two organizations embody this very dogma: Lima Company and The Citadel football program. Members of my team and my company possessed these qualities and upheld these values in spades.

In Lima Company, the chain of command is in charge of seventy cadets. That goes for every company in The Citadel.

"Wait, how many companies are there at The Citadel?" Mary interjected.

"Well, that's a good question. Hmmm… let me see… there are five battalions, four companies in each battalion—except for Second Battalion, which has the Band Company also—making a total of twenty-one."

"At the top of command in each company is the company commander. From there, it ranks down into cadet leadership. The second-highest rank in our company is the company XO, then it goes down the list of senior officers, senior privates, first sergeant, squad sergeants, junior privates, clerks, corporals, sophomore privates—and then of course, lastly, knobs. This network of cadets must work in unison for anything to get done. Each rank-holder has a specific job he or she must attend to on a regular basis."

"What was the highest rank you had?"

I laughed. "Well, like I told you before, my main two focuses were school and football. I honestly did not care to earn rank. At times it seemed like a fun thing to do; however, if I was going to graduate in three years and be a starter for the football team, I didn't have time to take on more responsibility, so the highest rank I ever had at The Citadel was senior private. Yep, I made it all the way up to the top tier of rank. Well, of course that's behind the senior officers."

Having rank is great experience for anyone who wants to take on the responsibility of being a manager. The skills you will cultivate in a ranked position are directly transferable to those of the civilian world. Anytime you have a chance to assume a position of leadership, I say go for it. "Well then, why didn't *you* do it?" Mary asked, looking up at me earnestly.

"I wanted to. However, I just had different priorities. Looking back on it, I wish I had."

Like Lima, The Citadel football team had a chain of command as well. At the top of the command was our head coach, followed by the defensive coordinator and the offensive coordinator, the individual position coaches, the player's council, the team captains and the players.

In order for our team to be successful, trust was essential. If I didn't trust that our defensive coordinator was calling the right play and, as a result of my doubt, attempted something outside of my responsibility, our defense would fall apart. All it took was one person to screw up his assignment and the other team would score six points.

In addition to trust, a sense of duty for the team was also important. In Lima Company, every cadet had the duty to keep his or her room and personal appearance on par with The Citadel standard, and it was the duty of the platoon leaders and sergeants to make sure this was being done. If a cadet failed to do his or her duty, then he or she got assigned to cons, which meant he or she had to sit in his or her room (like a child's time out), or tours, which meant he or she had to walk back and forth on the quad with a rifle. It was the same in football. If a player jumped offsides, missed an assignment, or just didn't do what he was supposed to do, then he would be doing sprints, barrel rolls, or bear crawls at the next practice.

Other duties of a cadet included Friday parades, Saturday-morning inspections, attending home football games, attending company meetings, going to regimental PT at 5:30 a.m., participating in rifle draw, taking company pictures, going to counseling, attending class, and sitting guard duty in the front sally port of Law Barracks about once every two months or so. I didn't mind any of those duties; however, sitting guard duty was the most boring job ever. Some guys in my company literally bribed others to sit guard duty for them just to get out of it.

"How long did you have to do it for?"

"Usually until the next meal. For instance, if I had guard duty at the beginning of the day, I would be there until lunch.

"Oh, what is the point of that?" Mary asked.

"Because we couldn't let anyone inside the barracks who was not a cadet."

"Why not?"

I laughed. "Only cadets were allowed inside the barracks. We couldn't let strangers into our personal dorms, especially because we had rifles in there as well."

"Y'all had guns?" she asked, looking amazed.

"Technically, yes. We did. They were missing some key parts, though—the parts that allow them to fire."

All cadets—male, female, athlete, knob, officer, or part of The Summerall Guard—had similar duties. Nevertheless, despite this fact, there seemed to be a sense of resentment from the non-athletes against members the Corps Squad (the student athletes). It is true that we missed things others were required to attend. It is true that our physical appearance sometimes was not up to par, and we weren't as strict about the dress code. But what the non-athletes may not have appreciated was that we sometimes missed things because we had other duties to tend to such as mandatory practices, lifts, and meetings. In addition to the regular rigors of The Citadel, we had the rigors of football to contend with. We had to maintain a certain weight and keep our bodies in tip-top shape. We actually had more on our plates than non-athletes did. That's probably why we didn't check our emails as regularly as the non-athletes did and thus were sometimes unaware of changes or important messages until it was too late.

In any case, the gap between the regular Corps and the Corps Squad has narrowed a lot since General Rosa's tenure and the hiring of Captain Geno Paluso as the commandant. Paluso came in as the new commandant in 2014. He strategized with some of the coaching staff and TAC officers to come up with a plan to bring the distinct cultures of Corps Squad and Corps closer together. It all started by letting people see the other person's viewpoint—specifically, letting the Corps know that members of the Corps Squad were not simply sloughing off their duties. Somehow the message was disseminated and the cultures started merging. Remarkably, something as simple as basic communication brought our school together like never before.

Football and the Corps are similar. Both are highly structured organizations with strict rules. Just as the Corps mandates morning room inspections, the football team mandates locker room inspections. The idea is to instill discipline in every aspect of our lives, thereby taking care of the small stuff so that we can truly make an impact on the big picture. Micro focus allows macro impact. My best academic semesters were when I was in season. I didn't have time to dwell or waste on other things. Structure, provided by football and The Citadel, is a great tool to have and helped me stay on track.

I have talked about everything needed to be a successful leader except for the most vital characteristic: respect. A coach must respect his players in order for his players to respect him. An officer must respect his cadets in order for his cadets to respect him. It is because of respect that we follow rules, hold each other accountable and do our due diligence to accomplish a common goal. Respect doesn't only apply to people. We also respect offices and institutions. My respect for The Citadel is based off its core values and academic curriculum. It is because of this respect that I was proud to wear the cadet and football uniforms. I think about all of the men who wore that uniform before me, of the tradition held in this institution. It is a standard to be clean shaven, with shined shoes and brass, and military creases in my uniform. I respected that it was a privilege to be a cadet at this college.

Respect starts with respecting yourself. Once you respect yourself, then respecting others comes naturally. The backbone of respecting yourself is being completely honest with who you are. That involves simply being true to yourself. They say a person of integrity acts the same way even knowing they would not get caught. If you don't have integrity, it's hard to respect yourself.

Lastly, to be a leader you must be adept at dealing with adversity. Adversity is anything but rare in an environment such as The Citadel. Adversity *is* The Citadel. Whether it's an assignment given through the chain of command, from a coach, or even from a professor, just find a way to do it. There are no buts in doing so. The most important aspect of this part is to take control of the situation and move on. F.I.D.O. "F@%$ it, Drive On" is a phrase quite often spoken in this institution. If you can't do anything about the situation or problem, then there's no reason to dwell on it. Complete what you need to and move on to the next assignment.

"Don't count the days,
make the days count."

\- MUHAMMAD ALI

Chapter 8:

THE BAND OF GOLD

"Can you tell me about how you got the ring now?" Mary said, glancing down at my band of gold. Ah… the band of gold. Alumni say that it's worth is more than any other single piece of jewelry ever sold.

"Yes, Mary. I will," I said solemnly. "And first, let me tell you, there's much more than just what you see here."

This ring tells a story. The band of gold is much more than just a class ring. At other colleges, such as Alabama or Georgia Southern, a class ring is a symbol of various academic achievements; however, at this great institution some would say that it means something greater than a diploma. As I told you earlier, The Citadel is not like most schools. Of course, it's a military academy, and that makes it unique in and of itself. It's devoid of the party atmosphere. Students don't spend half their time drinking and partying and only stressing out right before their exams. (I'm not knocking my friends who went to those schools; I'm just saying that I wouldn't want to wear a ring that represented that sort of accomplishment. I'm proud of the discipline I acquired at The Citadel.)

Another way The Citadel is different is that it's much smaller than other Division I public universities. A great example is UGA, where the student enrollment hovers around 60,000. That means UGA's a road well-traveled. I'm not saying graduating from UGA is not an accomplishment. Being able to get a college degree at all is a huge accomplishment. I'm just trying to show you, the reader, another unique characteristic about my great institution. Only 60,000 people have ever graduated from The Citadel since the school's founding in 1842, and among these 60,000 there are many great and successful men and women who have made a real difference in the world.

The ring I wear is not a token for the faint of heart; nor will it ever be worn by those that do not understand the adversity pertaining to the achievement of being able to have such a high esteem. I'm not bragging; I'm just boasting about how great a school The Citadel is.

The high esteem for The Citadel is not arrogance, but fact. How many students outside of military academies know what it is truly like to have discipline? To wake up every morning before the sunrise, to make your bed, to iron your uniform, to shine your brass and shoes, to go to formation all before you have to march to breakfast, go to morning classes, march to lunch, and go to afternoon classes, then go off to meet for football meetings, workouts, practice, eat dinner, and spend a couple of hours studying before going to bed at midnight only to wake up the next morning to repeat the same process? But my ring represents more to me than just a disciplined routine. It also holds within it many memories, both positive and negative. It's a daily reminder of how truly blessed I am to be on this earth and to have been able to play the sport I love for sixteen years; how blessed I am to even be able to go to school and get a great education, and to have an opportunity to one day make a tremendous difference in the world. I mean hopefully I am making a difference in your life as you listen to my story. It's crazy, but just one life can have a tremendous impact. Look at Martin Luther King Jr., Mother Teresa, and Jesus Christ. Just ask yourself: How can I make a difference? Let it come to you and when it does, go out and do it. Life is too short to just watch it go by and be but a number in a world full of them. You only live once, so go out and live! Follow your passion and follow your dream.

"The history of the band of gold dates back to the Civil War era. Did you know that The Citadel is the first college to ever fire on our government? You see, back in those times the United States was going through a civil war."

"A what war?" Mary asked.

"Honey, I'll tell you more about that later on. Don't interrupt his story," said her mom.

"No, it's fine. I enjoy the curiosity and engagement. The band of gold dates back to the start of the Civil War when shots were fired at Fort Sumter and continues all the way to the present, being worn by Mayor of Charleston Joseph Riley. Through all those years, the legacy of what it means to be a Citadel cadet has endured. To all those who have gone to the next life, those that wear the ring, and those that will one day in the future be bearers of the ring, I say congratulations for taking the road less traveled. You will join a tradition of saying what every person who ever went to The Citadel says, 'I wear the ring.'"

The way I received my ring was a little different from the normal procedure for receiving the band of gold. Traditionally, senior cadets receive their rings in the first semester of senior year. That's when The Citadel holds its annual ring ceremony (which we refer to as Ring Night). And like everything else at The Citadel, there are a bunch of ceremonies leading to the culmination of the ring ceremony. For example, there's the senior walk to all the bars in downtown Charleston on Wednesday night and a ritual where we drink champagne and break the glass on the quad with our company mates. Unfortunately, I wasn't able to participate in these ceremonies. In order to graduate early I had to make a couple of sacrifices, and that was one of them.

I received my ring during the sixth semester of my academic undergraduate career. Yep, this was my last semester as a cadet. With being on a full athletic scholarship and only having a year and a half left of eligibility, the only way I could get my MBA paid for was by graduating early. Thank God for Kate helping me set up my academic schedule and giving me the resources to be successful in the classroom. The Ring Ceremony and Ring Day are memories I will never have. However, the only way I could achieve my goal of graduating with a master's degree debt free is through the path I chose.

Mary was not satisfied with my story. She wanted details. "Can you tell me how you got it, though?"

Oh yes, of course. It was a Tuesday. I'll never forget this day because it was my dad's fifty-sixth birthday, March 3, 2015. It was an unseasonably warm day—summerlike, in fact, which in Charleston means hot and humid. It was after lunch, around 12:45 p.m., when I opened the email sent from Second Lieutenant O'Brien, USMC Class Ring Program Coordinator at The Citadel Alumni Association. "Ring has Arrived" was the subject line of the email. Just seeing those words filled me with joy. My hands started to sweat. "Let's go!" I yelled aloud as I opened the message: "Your ring has arrived at the Alumni Center. Please arrange for a time to pick up your ring. Thanks."

Class started in fifteen minutes, which didn't give me much time to make it to the Alumni Center, but I didn't care. There was no way I'd be able to concentrate in class knowing my ring was sitting in the alumni office waiting for me, I reasoned, as I took off at a rapid two hundred and forty steps per minute. Since it was a hot day, I was soon drenched in sweat. My duty shirt had changed to a darker shade of gray and sweat was sliding down the side of my face. Reaching up, I realized that even the brim of my cap was completely soaked through. I didn't let this stop me, though, and dashed into the Alumni Office.

"Excuse me, Miss, is Second Lieutenant O'Brien here?" I asked the lady behind the reception desk.

"He's still on his lunch break. He should be back any moment now." Dang. What a piece of luck. I couldn't go back to campus without seeing my own ring. I'd been dreaming about receiving it ever since matriculation day. I could hardly believe the day was here, and now I was being stymied by O'Brien's lunch break. I decided right then and there: I had to get my ring, and I didn't care if I was late to class or not. They could give me the cons and tours—I didn't even care. This was one of the most important moments of a Citadel cadet's experience, and I was not going to miss out on it.

Luckily, O'Brien came in at 12:55 p.m.

"Excuse me, Second Lieutenant? I received an email today saying that my ring order arrived, and I would like to pick it up." I gave him my name and he glanced at a list on his desk and then turned to the boxes of rings piled up next to it. "Crochet... Crochet.... Ah! Here it is. Cadet Crochet, Lima Company." He handed over this wooden box with The Citadel school logo on the top. I opened it up. With much excitement and gratitude to God for giving me this once-in-a-lifetime opportunity, I opened the box and gazed upon the most beautiful ring I had ever seen. On it was the number 15—representing the class of 2015—even though I was, technically, a member of the class of 2016. (In order to graduate early, I had to get a ring with a 15 instead of a 16.)

I picked up it out of the box. It was heavier than I had expected. I looked at it for what felt like seconds but was more likely minutes. All Citadel rings look the same on the outside: on one side it said "The Citadel" in raised letters, with a bullet, a bow, and a sword and rifle crossing each other. On the other side were Big Red, Old Glory, a star, two guidons, and six cannon balls. Inside the ring was my custom engraving: "Don't count the days, make the days count. JEC (my initials for Joseph Edward Crochet) Lima '16." Even though my ring on the outside says 2015, I want my classmates and company mates from Lima to know that I will always be a member of the class of 2016.

I had selected this quote because it got me through my darkest hours at The Citadel and helped me obtain my goals. My parents always taught me the importance of giving your best and making the most out of everything that comes your way, each and every day. The importance of not taking a day for granted is something I value and contemplate every morning when I first wake up. I'm not one to waste a day. Each one of us was put on this earth for a certain amount of time, a set number of days. Everyone has the same twenty-four-hour opportunity in which to make the most of each day, regardless of what that day brings them. They may be thrown off course by unexpected obstacles; things might not always go as planned due to forces beyond our control (or due to our own lapses in judgment, even). This is to be expected. What's important is not to lose focus. With vision and focus and perseverance, you will ultimately succeed. You must be determined to improve—albeit only by one percent—every single day. Keep chipping away at your goals! Many people have asked me how I could graduate in only three years while playing a Division I sport. I tell them the truth: it wasn't easy; I just kept believing that I could do anything I put my mind to doing.

I'd always wanted to be able to say "I wear the ring." Seeing Coach Drayton and Coach Standard, my high school football head coach, wearing the very same ring that I wanted every time I saw them motivated me even more. The moment had finally arrived. Now the only thing left for me to do was to finish the semester and to walk across the stage to receive my diploma.

"*All our dreams can come true, if we have the courage to pursue them.*"

- WALT DISNEY

Chapter 9:

GRADUATION

After receiving my ring, the rest of the semester flew by. All of us who would be graduating were eagerly counting down the days until May 9, 2015. Countless hours spent going to classes, studying, working on projects, and taking exams were finally going to pay off. The only rituals still separating me from graduation were a baccalaureate Mass, the long Gray Line Parade, and a three-hour graduation ceremony.

The day of the baccalaureate Mass, I walked into Summerall Chapel and spotted my mom, dad, and Emily seated among a very small congregation. Because the baccalaureate Mass is a Catholic ceremony, there weren't many people in the chapel. I remember thinking that if I had known the baccalaureate Mass was optional, I would have gone out to party instead! I took a seat in one of the middle pews. Emily and my parents were sitting in the side pews, facing me to show their support.

This was my second-ever baccalaureate Mass, and I enjoyed it a lot more than I did the high school one. It had nothing to do with the mass or the homily; rather, it had everything to do with the people with whom I was seated. After Mass, my dad reminded me that I only had to get through one more parade and one more ceremony, and then I would be a Citadel alumnus. I loved the way that sounded. The next day would be my final day marching in a cadet uniform with the entire student body.

The Long Gray Line Parade kicked off at 2:00 p.m. All the seniors locked arms and started walking toward First, Second, and Third Battalion across Summerall Field. As we were walking, I couldn't help but think about my first parade during my freshman year. Something that stuck out in my mind about that first parade was overhearing a cadet in my company who was a year older than me denigrating my status as athlete. Here I was graduating a year early—with his class, in fact—and he wasn't even present, having been kicked out somewhere along the line due to an honor violation. Oh, the irony!

As I was marching, I saw my family, my friends, and even my aunts and uncles in the crowd of observers. I was the first grandson and nephew to graduate from college on my mom's side of the family. It was such an honor. As I continued walking, I looked at Second Battalion and at the large face of the clock on the center tower. I looked up at the sky and saw big fluffy clouds and birds flying overhead. I was ecstatic.

Graduating meant the world to me, but I knew it meant even more to my parents, who had worked their butts off raising me and my brother. I knew they were proud; their faces were beaming. I will always remember their faces.

My advice to you is please always live life the right way. The hard route is not as appealing as the easy route; however, in the long run it's so much more enjoyable and you will always be rewarded for doing good. As my favorite public speaker, Inky Johnson, said, "The process is more important than the product." It's about taking pride in what you do. When you look in the mirror, can you say to yourself that you did all you could do? Did you embrace the process and use your circumstances as opportunities to bless other people? Hopefully I am doing so by writing this book. I mean, I have put hundreds of hours into writing this manuscript with the hope that it will help others.

"Tell me about graduation!" Mary interrupted me.

"Okay, okay."

The time finally came. Graduation day. Saturday, May 9, 2015. I woke up at 5:00 a.m.

I arrived on campus at 7:00 a.m., wearing my full dress. (I called it the George Washington outfit, since it looked like a uniform one of our founding fathers would have worn two hundred and fifty years ago.) Graduating seniors lined up in front of Deas Hall to be checked in by Sergeant Green. Sergeant Green was notorious for checking every minute detail of every cadet's personal appearance. I stood in line for about fifteen minutes, too happy to even care about other distracting matters. Before I knew it, Sergeant Green stood before me. "What's going on, High Speed?"

"Nothing much, Sergeant Green. I'm just ready to walk across that stage."

He smiled at me with a sinister look. "Not so fast. You're gonna have to get that hair in order one last time."

There were two barber shops inside Deas Hall, so I hurried in for a trim. Really all they did was clean up the edges, and I felt victorious for having scored a free haircut. I also looked sharp for the ceremony and subsequent photos.

Inside the gym, we gathered in alphabetical order and socialized. There were people in line with me whom I wish I had gotten to know better. There were others, like Ty, whom I knew very well. It was pretty awesome to be graduating with Ty, I thought, feeling a bit nostalgic. After all, he and I had played on the Tucker Lions football team together way back in the sixth grade. And look at us now!

After about an hour General Rosa, along with faculty and staff, took their places in front of us, and the pomp and circumstance began. I had never seen McAlister Field House so filled with people! Row after row of smiling faces watched us march into the gym. I sat at the front right, facing the stage, as General Rosa and a couple others addressed our class. What really stole the show, though, was the speech of the 2015 commencement speaker, Dr. Keller Kissam (Class of 1988). Before Dr. Kissam spoke, he was introduced by General Rosa as the Senior Vice President, SCANA Corporation President, Retail Operations South Carolina Electric & Gas Company.

Dr. Kissam's words were so moving to me that I've reprinted his commencement address in its entirety here:

(Applause)

Mr. Kissam speaking: "General and Mrs. Rosa, General Watts, members of The Citadel board of visitors, honored guests, staff, faculty, friends, family, but most importantly you, the graduating class of 2015 of the South Carolina Corps of cadets. It is my highest honor and most unique privilege to be here today to share in your commencement exercises. The world's waiting on you. It's waiting to gobble you up and spit you out. Dash your hopes and shatter your dreams. In the opening monologue of the movie Patton, George C. Scott exclaims Americans love a winner and will not tolerate a loser. My how things have changed. Just pick up the magazine or newspaper and read the headlines. Americans are infatuated with failure and mesmerized with falls from grace. Our heroes have been regulated to the small print and section c or the last five minutes of the nightly news. Benign headlines, human interests. What?! You didn't think you'd get such words of encouragement and promise on this your special day?

"Well, don't sweat it! Four and a half years ago you made a decision that will equip you to not only handle it, but to flourish. Know this, your degree that you receive will mean more to you given global circumstances and events than it has meant to any alumnus who has preceded you. The core values of your education—honor, duty, respect—coupled with the progression of prepare, serve, lead, and command will serve as your compass. A rudimentary but effective tool. It will tell you always where you have been, where you are, but most importantly where you are headed.

"Socrates said that the best way to live with honor in this world is to be the person you pretend to be. The most important words encrypted on this campus are above Summerall Chapel. Ecclesiastes 'Remember now thy Creator in the days of thy youth.' Honor your blessings, for you are blessed to be here today.

"You got health, you got vitality, you got youth. Honor those blessings. Stay in shape or get in shape. Life's too complicated to have to worry about your health and watch what you put in your body. The headlines across the country of young people your age who have met a fatal end because of a toxic dose of alcohol or drugs. Be careful what you put in your body and understand that your career, your future, your life is not worth getting to the bottom of a twelve-ounce can or half-gallon bottle.

"I now ask the parents of these graduating seniors to now rise and be recognized."

(APPLAUSE)

"Honor your parents. They're the reason you are here. They've got so much invested in you and it's not just tuition, but it's unconditional love and support. Be worthy of that investment. I was here four years ago when you all joined the Corps of Cadets. I watched *as they craned their necks trying to find you as you marched from those barracks to Summerall to matriculate into the Corps of Cadets. I saw that same sense of pride going to every football game, and every parade ceremony, and I see that same pride on all their faces here today. They gave you something more important, your last name! Honor it!*

"Like my good buddy Dorris Bentley says, 'Passed down from generation, too far back to trace, I see all my relations. I look into my face—may never make it famous, but I'll never bring it shame. It's my last name.... it's my last name.'

"Honor those parents and honor your family. I learned the importance of family back in 2004 when we had an ice storm that came through our service territory. Had 155,000 customers who didn't have power. And the most important thing in my life was getting those lights back on. I didn't go home for a week. I didn't talk to my wife, my son, or my daughter because the most important thing in my life was my job.

"Like always, after about a week we got the lights back on. I was feeling good because I had just accomplished the most important thing in my life—once again, my job. I remember sleeping through the Super Bowl that Sunday. Going to work on Monday. My phone ringing incessantly. Irritated, I stepped out in the hallway to answer the call and saw it was my wife Ann. I said what do you want? She was crying on the other end. You need to come to Rich Memorial Hospital right now.

"I said are you ok? She said it's not me it's Elliot. Elliot at the time was my six-year-old daughter. Two and a half hours later I sat in front of a pediatric oncologist who told me that seventy percent of the cells in her bloodstream were cancerous. She was diagnosed with leukemia. And I can promise you at that particular moment I

didn't care if anybody in the state of South Carolina had power or would ever have it again. It's never been my highest priority but I can tell you this... after that one day I have never had a bad day in the office. Honor your parents; honor your family. That's what gives your life meaning.

"And finally honor this institution. Today after you walk across this stage you will be joining a tradition that has been in place since 1842. And our institution's reputation is not defined by its charter of incorporation but by the actions and contributions of its Alumni. When I am in a meeting and people look over and see my ring and say 'Oh, you went to The Citadel?' it makes me proud. But what makes me even prouder is when they never see my ring and ask me 'Where did you go to school?' And I say The Citadel and they say 'Oh... I should have known.'

"Honor this institution.

"The second most important words that are encrypted across this campus are in every sally port of the barracks. And that is 'Duty is the sublimest word in the English language.' For the last four years you lived underneath a regimented lifestyle. I will tell you: keep that regiment in your life. It will serve as a foundation and a stabilizer in a very chaotic world. Someone asked me would you go back to The Citadel and do knob year over again? And I think and say let me think a minute. I wouldn't have to make any decision about where I needed to be; I wouldn't have to make any decision about what I have to wear; I wouldn't have to make any decision about even what I was going to eat. Man, what a refreshing change. Sign me up. I'll see you in August."

(APPLAUSE)

"Keep that regiment in your life. In addition to that, follow the rules. One hundred percent compliance. That's why I am proud of Captain Paluso and General Rosa who are enforcing the rules of the fourth-class system. Not making any changes but enforcing the rules. Why? Because I can tell you why?

"Because when the Environmental Protection Agency, the Federal Regulatory Commission, the Department of Justice, when they come in and do audits of my company, they don't come in to audit the rules I feel like following. It's one hundred percent of the rules and as a leader you have a duty to be compliant one hundred percent. In addition to that you have a duty to understand you're going to make mistakes. We all do but you need to be accountable at those times. Don't whine, don't complain, don't make excuses, and my favorite—don't call somebody to bail you out. When you make a mistake, don't get bitter—get better. Forget about it and move on."

(Applause)

"Duty is indeed the sublimest word in the English language, but it is followed closely by discipline, accountability, and persistence. And then finally you got to earn respect as a leader. You have to earn respect. Two types of leaders: those that have position power and those that have people power. Your senior class president alluded to that moments ago. Those people that just have position power, they take off their rank; they throw their business card away and don't have much respect because it only comes with the title that they have somehow earned. But you got to earn it through people-power. Be a servant leader. Responsible for your people and indirectly responsible for the welfare of their families. People come to me and they ask me what do you look for in a leader to promote

in your company? I said that is so easy. Two things: Number one, how do they treat people who can't do a dang thing for them? And the second thing is their judgment. Good judgment. I would rather have somebody working for me with average intelligence that uses good judgment one hundred percent of the time than to have someone who is brilliant and uses good judgment fifty percent of the time.

"As a leader you earn respect by being a good communicator. Open and honest communication. Technology is overrated. Communication is hand to hand, face to face, eyeball to eyeball."

(Applause)

"I know if we threw everything in a bucket we probably would have more electronic devices in here then we do people. But it's overrated. I'm a firm believer. I never have been on Facebook and I am a firm believer that if you go out and tell two hundred of your friends that you are going to the beach for a week and you post selfies confirming that you are there, you deserve to have your house broken into and get your things stolen.

"Use discretion. But people don't communicate because it takes time and everybody is busy. It takes effort and we have a lazy streak and we all run the risk of confrontation when we communicate. But stand up and be a good leader and communicate openly and honestly.

"And then, finally, as a leader to earn respect make a decision. Efficiently gather your facts but people are looking at you to be decisive. Across corporate America today nobody can make a decision without a team, committee. I call it the meet-and-eat crowd because that seems to be all they do. Gather your facts and make a decision. When you make that decision, enforce it firmly, fairly, and consistently.

Remember this: Respect is like a boomerang; the harder you throw it at somebody else, the quicker it will come back to you. So today you leave the freshly cut grass of Summerall field. That distinctive smell of the pluff mud of the Ashley River and the familiar laughter of your classmates. Never again will you have to get a shirt stay and try not to bounce when you march. But you will never forget that appearance and bearing matter. Never again will you bark out 'sir yes sir' or ma'am yes ma'am' while bracing on the galleries, but you will never forget that good manners and respect never hurt anyone. Never again will you walk in the gutter of the avenue of remembrance, but you will never forget that humility is a virtue. Never again will you instruct a knob on how to make a bed, how to shine shoes, or how to shine brass, but you will never forget that if you thoroughly know something, there is great pride in teaching it to others. Never again will you cram for an exam or clean you room for inspection, but you will never forget to be prepared in mind and resources. Never again will you spend Friday afternoon at parade or Saturday morning at inspection, but you will never forget how to do within while doing without and that sacrifice breeds confidence. Never again will you play another intramural game in Deas Hall or on Summerall Field, but you will never forget that teamwork is a critical element of achievement and fun. Never again will you march behind a Guidon flapping in the breeze as your company passes in review, but you will never forget that cohesion and coordination create an esprit de corps in any unit. Never again will you hear Reveille or Taps emanating from the guard room of Padgett Thomas Barracks, but you will never forget the value of taking the road less traveled. And never again will you sign in after leave, confirm all in or credit sources for a paper, but you will never forget the third most important words inscribed on this campus: 'You will never lie, cheat, steal nor tolerate those who do.'

"People ask what's the best thing that ever happened to you. A lot of people would say well it's the parents whom I was born to. Some will say it's the job or career that I get to fulfill each day. Some people will say it's the spouse that I was fortunate enough to marry. Others will say, surely, it's the kids that we were blessed to have. I tell you, without a doubt the greatest thing that ever happened to me was the opportunity to matriculate and receive an education here at The Citadel, The Military College of South Carolina, because it's made all of those other things that are important in my life have a deeper purpose and a greater meaning and that's my sincere wish for you.

"Remember this, you are my heroes... God bless you and congratulations."

-Dr. Keller Kissam, Class of 1988

His speech blew me away. It put life in perspective. I've already told you that throughout my whole life it had been a dream of mine to graduate from college, and now that dream was coming true. But what was next for me? Trepidation crept in. I had had structure, discipline, and my life planned out for me from my entire childhood up to this point, and now all that was coming to an end.

It got my mind rolling about the importance of choices. Everyone in today's world has the ability to make choices each day. They elect to do right or wrong. Too many people in our generation fail to realize the importance of choices or understand that there are consequences for every choice they make. All it takes is one bad decision to destroy the rest of your life. Too many times, I've seen great athletes and students get kicked out of The Citadel for making bad decisions. I believe most people are good at heart, but society judges us on our actions and decisions even if it is a simple context of being caught in the moment. Many people who started this journey with me on matriculation day were not there to walk across the stage with me today because of a single choice they made at some point along the way. I could have done the same. I could have smoked weed, gone drinking and driving, or even cheated on my tests, but every time I was tempted to do such a thing I remembered all the sacrifices I had made to get here and the values my parents had instilled in me at a young age. It's never worth sacrificing a dream or a goal for a simple short cut or a short-term buzz.

Following the commencement speech, I got out of my seat to follow in line to receive my diploma. As I was walking to the stage, I turned toward Emily, my brother, and my friends all sitting there and posed for a picture. After that, I continued to follow the line. I went up the stairs, shook Captain Paluso's hand, and then suddenly: "Cadet Joe Crochet, Magna Cum Laude" was announced. It was my turn to walk across the stage in front of everyone and receive my diploma: my bachelor's of science in business administration. I walked to General Rosa. He gave me a firm handshake and handed me my diploma. As we posed to take a picture he said, "Hey Joe, you still have some eligibility left, don't you?"

I smiled back at him, "Yes sir, I do. I still have two more seasons left."

"Two more? That's fantastic! I can't wait to see y'all this year. Y'all are going to be good."

After the ceremony it was time for photo taking, and believe me, we took dozens. In addition to my immediate family, my aunts, uncles, friends, and grandmother had attended. Nanny, my grandmother, was so proud to have attended the commencement. In a weird coincidence, her husband (my grandfather) had died on the day I was born, so she has always felt a special connection to me.

After pictures, we proceeded to the beach house on Isle of Palms that my family had rented to celebrate the occasion. We partied for two days straight. We had champagne, beer, cake, hot dogs, burgers, mac and cheese, and my all-time favorite—my dad's gumbo! If you never have had the famous Crochet gumbo recipe—an old Cajun recipe passed down from generation to generation—I recommend that you try it. I will have that famous gumbo at every homecoming Citadel football tailgate from here on out. I can't promise there will be some for everyone, but I can promise I'll be eating it before going to cheer on the Dogs.

This weekend completed my era as a cadet at The Citadel; however, through the grace of God I still had two more football seasons left and graduate school. It was time to be a leader and turn this program around.

"I'll tell you what...that boy is tougher than a ten-cent steak."

- COACH PAUL STANDARD,
CLASS OF 1984

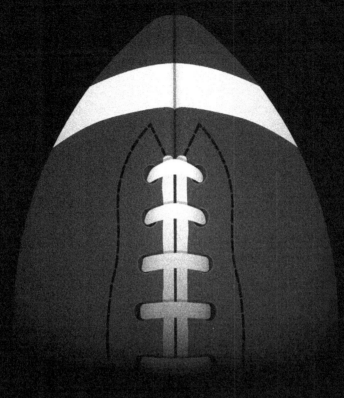

YEAR FOUR

Red-Shirt Junior Season

Chapter 10:

FALL CAMP

Though I was no longer a cadet, I still had a duty to be a Christian, to pursue my master's degree, to play football, and to keep my life in order. Putting and keeping your life in order is much easier said than done. I try to live each day like God would want me to, though sometimes I know that I fail. I don't fail at praying, though. I pray at least five times a day: in the morning when I first wake up, before each meal, and before I go to bed. Praying helps keep my faith alive, and that summer after graduation I did not know that my faith was about to be tested. I did not know that our team was going to need Jesus more than ever to save us during the hot and humid month of August when fall camp began.

The toughest part of fall camp was the rigorous schedule. We woke up at 6:00 a.m. and practiced football until 9:30 p.m. Playing the game at our level requires more reacting than thinking. It's bare instinct. All the thinking happens in meetings and preparation Monday through Friday. Come game time, you either know it or you don't. To be successful on the field, you must be able to put aside all distractions, line down, and compete. And in fall camp that's all we did—line down and compete! A lot of guys would say ranger school is tough, BUD/S training is tough. Hell—knob year is tough. Not taking anything away from those experiences, but I'd like to challenge you to think about two-a-days in full pads during the month of August in Charleston, South Carolina. It wears a person down mentally, physically, spiritually, and emotionally.

In the recent past, however, things have been changing. Nowadays there are restrictions and limitations on what NCAA players can do during practice. The game is changing completely because of knowledge gained from research on concussions and chronic traumatic encephalopathy. I must admit that I'm glad I am no longer playing; after playing the game for eighteen years and having experienced multiple concussions, I'm frightened to think about what might lie ahead for me.

On the first day of camp we met in Grimsley Hall Auditorium to go over all the paperwork and NCAA-compliance material needed before starting the season. Each of us was subjected to a routine physical check-up to make sure our bodies were healthy enough to play. I always have a hard time with my blood pressure. Andy Clawson said I have white coat syndrome, which means I would get nervous about having my blood pressure measured, and being nervous would make my blood pressure higher than normal. It used to take a couple of tries before my blood pressure would register in the normal range.

After multiple hours of meetings, we were finally sent to our rooms to get a good night's rest before the first day of practice. As I put my head on my pillow, I thought about how our bodies wouldn't be this healthy again until after December.

In the morning, I woke up and changed into my PT uniform. Even though I was no longer a cadet, all football players were required to wear PTs during camp. During camp, everyone stayed in their assigned room for the year and all the fifth-years (including me, a fourth-year) stayed in a room in First Battalion.

"What's a fifth-year?"

"Someone who's no longer a cadet but is still on the football team. Usually it's because they are red-shirt seniors, also known as fifth-year players. In this case it was Alex Glover, Mike Mabry, Brandon Eakins, and myself in the second large."

"What's a second large?"

"It's the corner room of a battalion. Ours was on the second floor, making it the second large. Even though I had two years of eligibility left, since I was no longer a cadet and in graduate school, I was treated as a fifth-year senior."

Anyway, about the PTs: Coach Houston wanted all the players to look alike because we were a team, not a group of individuals. Technically, it was against the white book for alumni and others to wear cadet uniforms to impersonate a cadet. Luckily, I had the band of gold on my hand, so if a cadet or TAC officer tried to stop me, all I would have to do is show the ring and keep walking.

The schedule for fall camp was brutal. The only good thing about it was that being so busy left little time for my mind to drift. The less thinking for me, the better. I wanted to stay focused on getting through the long hot days ahead of me. In addition to the 6:00 a.m. to 9:30 p.m. schedule, we had seven two-a-days and only one day with a break.

Keys to surviving and thriving during fall camp all have to do with taking care of yourself: proper hydration, adequate sleep, and good nutrition are instrumental to peak performance. I remember walking to mess one morning; for some reason I was thinking that it could be worse—at least I had my friends. You see, every morning our group of friends got together to eat breakfast. We called it the "Breakfast Club." It originally started when Moose—Preston Durham—was there back in 2013; however, even though he transferred to Clemson, the tradition stayed alive. We talked about anything and everything under the sun. One of our favorite topics was planning for the future. We all had dreams, and the thought of making them come true kept our mind off practice; momentarily at least.

The moment I took one step outside my room, my shirt was already drenched in sweat. Thank the Lord we had air conditioning! I don't know how those older generations could stay in the barracks without AC. Those were some tough SOBs. The wet heat is something that is inescapable. After mess, I walked to Seignious Hall to get ready for meetings and practice. We met in the team room at the beginning of every day—always on time or early. (Coach Houston's rule "If you're eleven or more minutes early, you are early; if you're ten minutes early you're on time; and if you're on time you are late" is not something to mess with.)

Coach Houston addressed us with any news or issues he had from the previous day's practice and gave us pointers to focus on for the upcoming practice.

"We need more intensity," he began. "Our goal is to win the SoCon. That is it. You won't win it unless you properly believe it. This crap about having a winning season is pointless. We play the game to win, and by golly we are playing to be the best team in the Southern Conference. Point blank period. I need more intensity from both sides of the ball today. You think Davidson, Western Carolina or Wofford are gonna let you beat them with that effort out there?"

The goal every year I had been there had been to win a SoCon championship, but this was the first time I had heard it verbalized. Why was that? Hadn't everybody had the same goal of winning a SoCon championship? That's what I had always assumed. (But you know what they say about assuming—it makes an ass of u and me.)

118

Every great coach knows that a kid can be taught the best technique and proper methods to be a great athlete, but he can't coach effort. Effort is as plain as day to measure on the football field. You're giving it your all each and every play, or you're not. There was no point in trying to fake it; the truth would show up on film. Every morning we would watch the film as a team or in our position groups, and you'd better believe that Coach Houston would call out the players who didn't put forth sufficient effort. There was no excuse not to give one hundred and ten percent to every play you could.

The difference between Coach Houston's coaching staff and the previous coaching staff was that Coach Houston was not afraid to pull your scholarship if you weren't showing effort or doing what you are supposed to do either on or off the field. A great coach is a great leader who will inspect what he expects. In 2015, our expectations were high, and if you were not somebody that was going to help us achieve our goal of a SoCon championship, Coach Houston would make sure that you were not on the team for much longer. Having just one unconvinced player on the team could be a cancer in the locker room. To succeed, everyone had to have one hundred percent faith in their teammates, to trust that they would each do their jobs, and to trust that we all shared the common goal of being the first class since 1992 to win a SoCon championship. There had only been two Conference championships in the entire history of the school. We needed to change that! We had an opportunity to be the third!

After the team meeting, we broke into sides of the ball. Our (the defense's) persona was that we were vigilantes with an attitude and played the game with a chip on our shoulders. We were always arriving to the ball with a bad attitude. Coach Drayton walked in. "Fellas, fellas, what's going on? How are y'all feeling? I do not have to reiterate what the boss man said. We just need to go out there, be assignment sound, and whoop our offense's ass." We went over a couple of plays from the previous practice. Coach highlighted the good, the bad, and the ugly. He made sure that we all knew there was a standard and that we kept it.

"Fellas, do you know which ring is the most important ring is to have at this school?" Coach Drayton asked us. I looked down at my band of gold, and Coach Drayton took this as an answer.

"Wrong," he shouted. "Yes, of course The Citadel class ring is a special ring, and it's a privilege to wear it; however, there are tens of thousands of alumni that have that ring, so it is not the most important. The most important ring to have on this campus is a Citadel football Southern Conference championship Ring. Only two hundred men in the history of the entire school have one. This dates to the early 1900s, when football was first introduced to The Citadel. There have only been two conference championships at this school in over one hundred twenty years..." That got our entire defense thinking. James, Tevin, Mitchell, Mark, Nick, Dee, and I were not going to let our defense be on a team that was just going to have another season blow away in the wind.

After the defensive meeting, we broke up to go into position meetings. In Coach Weaver's meeting room, anything and everything goes. There were about nine of us: Me, Dondray, Q, Russell, Noah, Za'Von, Adam, Taylor, and Reid. We reviewed practice: Inside run, offense versus defense, half-line, and one-on-ones. The most important aspect of any meeting is drilling fundamentals. For me, the most important fundamental for my position was my first step. As a standup defensive end and outside linebacker, I needed to make sure I was in the best position to take a good first step. A good first step was crucial for properly reacting to a play and for being successful at my assignments. Position meetings lasted about an hour. We watched film, drilled fundamentals, highlighted improvements, and then went over the practice schedule for the day.

After the meetings were over, we had ten minutes to put on our shoulder pads, helmet, and cleats and be out on the field ready for warmups. The coaches only gave us two minutes until they came into the locker room, blowing their whistles and shouting at us to hurry up.

"We got a Conference to win!" one of them shouted.

We jogged out of Seignious to Wilson Field, The Citadel practice field. Coach D was already out there with his trunk box blasting loud, pump up music. All the camera crews were at their stations ready to film practice; the team managers and sports medicine staff were out there too. My buddy Drew was one of the best equipment guys on the staff. Unfortunately, he had to quit football after freshman year due to shoulder injuries, but he managed to make it as a member on the team another way.

As for the other team faculty, each position coach had a part of the field designated for pre-practice warm ups. Coach Weaver claimed the twenty-yard line on the right side of the field for us. I jogged to meet up with the rest of the guys. It must have been over a hundred degrees out there. We started by doing a light stretch, followed by practicing our first step footwork. After that, Coach Drayton called the defense together and we practiced formation and alignment with the scout team. This was for play recognition and to help our mental focus so we could just react come game time.

Ten minutes passed by and then all of a sudden, a whistle sounded. "All right, all right, all right. Y'all know what time it is," Coach D hollered as we jogged to form up in our stretching lines in the end zone. Coach D led the warmups. The music from the "funk trunk," was blasting. It usually played rap, but sometimes a little rock or country came on too. Either way, it helped pump us up to take on the day.

There were two ways to look at practice. The first was a pessimistic point of view, thinking that practice is about to suck and you just have to make it through. The other—a more optimistic approach, which is more conducive to making you become a great player—is viewing each practice as an opportunity to get better.

I was one of the eight players leading a line for warmups. In my line we had all of the Kats (linebackers) and some defensive linemen. We started the warmup by going in increments of twenty yards down and twenty yards back, doing lunges, side shuffle with arms, a-skips, runners' lunges, high knees, walking spider, backwards reverse lunge, backward hip skips, and other dynamic stretches. After the warmup, Coach D blew the whistle two times and we jogged onto the field from the end-zone for static stretching. I took my line to the forty-yard line, and every five yards behind me was where the next player in line fell until we hit the goal line. We stretched for fifteen minutes. Now that we were warmed up, it was show time.

We gathered as a team on the fifty-yard line. James did the gathering: "Where my dawgs at?" he bellowed, and we took off to our stations.

The first station up after warmups was none other than pursuit drill—the worst drill on the schedule. The nice thing about pursuit drill was that we could knock it out of the way at the beginning of practice. The shitty part about pursuit drill was that it physically drained us and was only the first period of practice. We had a decision to make: Dig deep and try to find a pair to make it through the rest of practice, or say "I got this" and thrive the rest of practice. Only SoCon championship teams thrive in practice, and that was what we wanted to be, especially since Coach had told us to focus more on our intensity and effort. That we had to have to have a great practice was a no-brainer.

Our team's mentality was that we were going to get at least one percent better each day. Nobody was going to stop us from achieving our goal, and we owed it to ourselves to attain it. After all, we were finally members of the senior class, hence leaders of the team. It was *our* team and we could make a huge difference. We had to win the day—each and every day.

(Whistle blows) stance, alignment, assignment, keys, and first step. SAAKF is the acronym…everything you needed to do before the snap. Be in a good stance and alignment to properly play your assignment. Through formation recognition and watching film, I could pick out what plays the other team might run and visualize my assignment for each play. As a defensive end and outside linebacker hybrid, my key was the offensive tackle. I based my first step off what he decided to do. The main thing was that on a down block, I had to be able to set a quick edge, to play the quarterback, and not to give anything up inside of me.

My gap was the C-gap on a base defensive play. My high school coach, Jerry Stewart, a hall of fame defensive coordinator for Parkview High School, Tucker High School and St. Pius X always said, "It's not where you line up, but where you wind up." In other words, do whatever you need to before the snap, but once that ball is hiked, you need to make sure you are where you need to be and doing your assignment that play.

After pursuit drill, we broke into our position groups for tackling drills, footwork drills, and ball drills.

I love hitting drills and always have, ever since Tucker Football League. There's something about putting all my force into another person. It relieves so much stress and aggression. At Tucker Football League, we used to practice for two hours, three days a week; and— I'm not kidding you—we did hitting drills for a total of three hours a week and conditioning for another three hours. If you played for the

Tucker Lions, you knew how to hit and run. There is a Hall of Fame wall there at that park with hundreds of names of former players that went on to play college football. It is a great program for developing top tier athletes.

I never had a practice tougher than a Tucker Lions football practice until I started playing football at The Citadel. During fall camp, the coaches loved making sure that we were physical and got after it. In other words, we went live with full pads and tackled to the ground every day. If it were any other college, we would only wrap up or would not even hit at all. But not at The Citadel! Football at The Citadel is shut up or nut up time. It's always the best against the best. Men shine while boys creep into the shadows. Any person can call out another person to compete in the summer with Coach D; however, once those pads go on is when the true beast come out.

As a starter, I had to make sure that I was giving my best effort and doing everything to be the best at my position. It was a constant battle. Defensively, we were set. James and Tevin both delivered punches up the middle. Mitchell and Jon Jon stuffed the interior gaps and made sacks. Mitchell was an amazing athlete. He weighed three hundred pounds, was the strongest guy on the team, and ran a forty-yard dash in four point eight seconds. He could have easily been playing for Alabama if only he were a little taller. Mark and I were on the edge as quick pass rushers. Mark was the Von Miller of the team; he had an innate ability to rush past linemen and sack quarterbacks. I, on the other hand, was just physical, assignment sound, and fortunate enough to have Mark and Mitchell flushing out the quarterback. In the secondary, we had Dee as a shutdown corner covering any receiver that lined up against him. He talked a lot of junk but could back it up. He was like a prime-time Deion Sanders. There was no doubt in my mind that he would be playing on Sundays. On the other side, we had Mariel

Cooper—Coop—a fifth-year transfer from South Carolina State, who was also a shutdown corner. I had not had much time to get to know Coop, but my initial impression of him was that he was super-cool and more driven than anybody else I knew. I also knew that he had lost his brother, Destin, who had also planned to be on our team, in a car accident the summer before he transferred to The Citadel. Maybe it was this family tragedy that fueled Coop to be a beast on the field. I was always excited to watch him perform. He has a true why and played for his brother every rep.

At safety, we had Nick, four-year starter from Dunwoody High School and Diggy. Both guys could make unbelievable plays in the open field and bring the wood on any run play that got past the linebackers. Lastly, we had the outside linebacker squad—my own boys, Q and Dondray. They were fast and possessed exceptional hand-eye coordination skills. They were big enough to play linebacker and fast enough to cover receivers as a dropdown safety.

In previous seasons during practice, the offense and defense would brother-in-law each other. Not this year, however.

"What's brother-in-lawing?" Mary asked.

"It means going easier on each other during practice because they're starters. It's basically a truce so that neither one would have to do anything during a play in practice just to take a break."

Brother-in-lawing might have been okay in the past; however, that crap did not fly with this coaching staff. We went against the offense for multiple periods. It helped us as a defense to prepare for Charleston Southern and Wofford; however, the offense needed to go against us to perfect their timing.

Next, we broke into starters versus the scouts. We had a mixture of offensive formations from Davidson, Western Carolina, and Georgia Southern. They were the first three games of the season—we needed to prepare. After ten periods of working with the scout team, we gathered back together for special teams and then one last competition. Generally, we went third down versus the offense, but that day we were going offense versus defense on the goal line.

The whistle blew. "All right, I want to see some effort and intensity. Defense, you better stop them—and offense, you'd better score." Coach Houston was fired up. The offense had the ball on the five-yard line. They had four downs to go five yards. That would be very easy for our offense to do. We averaged over three yards a carry last season; however, that was only when they played against other teams' defenses.

Bragging rights for the day were on the line. "Down, set, hike!" Dom handed the ball off to Tyler. (Wham!) He was met by Mitchell for a stop at the line of scrimmage. Second and goal from the five-yard line. "Set, Hike!" Dom hiked the ball, faked the hand-off to Tyler and kept it. (Wham!) I hit him as he pitched the ball to Vinny. Vinny caught the ball and got tackled by Tevin for a gain of two. Third and goal from the three-yard line. "Set, hike!" Dom hiked the ball. Sam pulled toward Mark. Mark stepped up and hit Sam in the backfield, blocking up the intersection, giving Tyler no room to go. James came out of nowhere and filled the b-gap, hitting Tyler for a gain of two. Fourth and goal from the one-yard line. It all came down to this last play.

"Kick their ass, Dark Side" … "Stuff that hole, Mitch" … "Let's eat, Joe Cro" … "Where my dogs at, James?" … "Let me see what you got, Dee." All the players who were not on the field were cheering for the defense or the offense. "Come on, Weaves, one more play!" "You got this, Tyler!" "Punch it in, O!" The chirping and cheering for both sides got louder and louder. It was time to drown out the noise. "Down, Set!" Cam, starting running back from Alabama, was in motion toward the other side of the defense. "Hike!" Dom pitched the ball to Cam. As Cam reached to grab the ball--(Wham!) He was met by Dee Delaney in the backfield for a loss. Whistles blew… "Defense wins the day!"

It always felt good to stop the offense in practice in goal line situations. They were the toughest team to defend in low yardage situations. Every year, they were one of the top two rushing offenses in the SoCon and in the nation. All we did was run the ball. Either way, the point is that we stopped them. Coach called us up to gather on the field.

"All right, guys," he said. "A lot better practice today than yesterday. Still have some things we need to improve on, but I like the intensity we had today. Now y'all break it down and get out of here. I'll see y'all later this afternoon."

We broke into position groups. Coach Weaver said, "Guys, good practice overall today. We'll look over film and make the corrections needed, but in the meantime go shower, hydrate, and rest up."

We ran off the field back to the locker room. Outside Seignious Hall were tubs filled with ice water for us, the grimy players. There's no better feeling than getting into those ice tubs after practice on a steamy August day. At first the cold is shocking, but after a couple of seconds your body goes numb and relaxes.

After cooling off and rejuvenating my muscles in the ice bath, I hopped in the shower. Showering during the day is all but pointless during fall camp. We worked out three times a day and were constantly sweating in the Charleston heat. I knew that after lunch I'd be back out there doing more of the same stuff. I just made sure to rinse off and only really washed before bed.

Music was already blaring from the locker room. Michelle, the sports medicine assistant, was already warning us about it. "Y'all need to turn that music down. We have people trying to work in here." It's a tough situation having sports medicine right next to the football locker room, because the locker room is the place where the teammates get hyped and wild to de-stress from the outside world. Some might say it's more of a man cave than a locker room, especially with the new renovations and the installation of the new sound system. The players loved turning it up in there.

After rinsing myself in the shower, I headed to lunch at the mess hall. The food on the menu was Philly cheesesteaks, mixed vegetables, and rice. There was also a fruit bar and a fountain machine from which we replenish our electrolytes and sugars. (It's funny how students from other schools complain about their cafeteria when they have so many options and freedom to eat whatever they want. I will never understand that. At The Citadel you can eat what is on that day's menu or you can order from a takeout place that delivers. Eating enough is especially important for football players, who have much higher calorie requirements than non-athletes, yet I always got my fill in the mess hall.)

After lunch we had about an hour of downtime to relax before ramping it back up for meetings, more workouts, and a walkthrough.

That was pretty much the routine for the entire four weeks of fall camp. As you can tell, it was not easy. Fall camp separates people who play the game from people who merely love the game. No one likes practicing; however, if you don't practice, you won't get better, and you won't be prepared for game day. All I could think about was the upcoming Davidson game. We had to make a statement. We were a new team, a new program, and we were on a mission.

"Tough times don't last, tough people do."

-ROBERT SCHULLER

Chapter 11:

THE GAME IS WON OR LOST BEFORE THE FIRST PLAY

Everyone on the Bulldog team was fired up and ready to usher in the 2015 season. We'd been feeling like losers ever since the final game of last season when we beat VMI, but had a record of 4-7. It was an awful feeling to be known as losers for an entire year. I myself, along with everyone else on the team, had chips on our shoulders. The conference, along with every other college football fan in the country, considered us failures. This was unacceptable to me. We had to change the way the world perceived us, and we would start by taking it one game at a time.

I could feel it in the air. It would be our redemption year. This would be the last season for the Class of 2016, and we had one goal in mind: Win, win, and win! It would be our year. I remember Coach Higgins and his coaching staff talking about our class when he recruited us. He said, "The Class of 2016 is going to be the first class to win a conference championship at The Citadel since 1992." The moment he recruited us, he knew that our class was special. He, along with all of us, believed that we were going to be the group of guys that led The Citadel to a championship. The two things we had going for us were that we were the largest class recruited to The Citadel, and we were by far the most united as a team.

Our class was unique in its unity. While it is true that great players have gone through this program such as Keith, Derek, Chris, Ben, Terrell, Bay, Aaron, Brandon, Rah, Darien, Mike, Cass, and others, we were the first class where *everyone* truly bought into the process. We were a band of brothers: not just teammates, but family. When a person faces adversity in life, he or she either becomes a victim of circumstance or a product of success. After surviving the departure of Coach Higgins and his staff and adjusting to an entirely new football program coaching staff, athletic director, and media personnel, we had chosen to be successful. Each and every one of us on the team knew that this was our chance to be great.

We teammates hung out more outside of football than we did in the locker room. That is saying something! In the summer, Coach D set up team events, which helped us bond a lot; however, the true team bonding and development of relationships started with grilling out, partying, and socializing together at fun events. There is a formula to building strong relationships. First, establish trust and honesty. Next, start seeing everyone on the team as family. At the end of the day, brothers fight and argue, but I knew in my heart that I would never do anything to let any of my brothers down. The more we hung out together outside of the locker room, the stronger our relationships became. Our class truly embraced each other as brothers; that was the key to success. A brotherhood.

Of course, feeling like brothers and having unity and bonding and all that great stuff wouldn't mean anything to a football team whose goal is to win a championship if we couldn't perform effectively on game day. When your goal is to win, it's not how you start, but how you finish that matters. Having a great start, however, definitely helps. It gives you an advantage. When running a forty-yard dash, the first four steps an athlete takes determine the outcome of the sprint. Hip explosion and knee drive are key for a quick time. Another example is winning in a game. It is much easier to win a game when you are ahead by a large margin. It is very difficult to come back from being behind (unless you're the Patriots and playing my Falcons for Super Bowl LI —don't even get me started on that!).

Anyway, the most effective winning strategy is to not ever let yourself get behind. Don't count on having a Patriots-like miracle, because that sort of thing is very rare indeed. One precaution you can take to avoid falling behind is to start out strong right from the start. That's what my team members and I did that year. Our unity, our brotherhood, and our shared experiences gave us an edge.

This reminds me of an analogy used by Coach Drayton: The moment a fighter steps into the boxing ring, he should be sizing up his opponent. That's why the most important shot taken from a boxer is the first punch. The first punch says a lot to an opponent. It's a statement! I want my opponent to know I'm ready to kick his you-know-what! It shows whether or not I'm really prepared to dominate him. The most important aspect of the first punch is never to show your opponent that you're scared, timid, or afraid to take him on.

Coach Houston, Coach Drayton, Coach Weaver, and the rest of the coaching staff made it a point for us to have a knockout punch on the first hit. There was no way Davidson had trained as hard as we had the past summer. Our will to win was much greater than theirs; we just needed to make a statement and show the rest of the country what we were all about.

September 5, 2015, the day of our season opener against Davidson,

I slept in till nearly 8:00 a.m. We were at the Charleston Plaza Hotel, which was pretty nice, especially when compared to some of the other roach-infested places we'd been put up at before. One thing about this new coaching team—they treated us like Division I players!

I turned on Sports Center and tuned into College Game Day. Every year, one FCS program has a game broadcasted on College Game Day, and I've always dreamed of playing in that game. How sweet would it be if it were The Citadel versus another SoCon team at home at Johnson Hagood Memorial Stadium?

Soon it was time to head downstairs with my teammates to strategize. We watched film on the other team for about an hour in one of the hotel's meeting rooms, with the starters seated in front. Then Coach called a play for us to line up in and then each person by position told the room how he reacted to the play and what his assignment was supposed to be as the ball was being snapped.

Around 8:45 a.m. we boarded the bus back to campus for breakfast at mess hall. Since our game wasn't until much later in the day, I filled up on a little bit of everything on the menu: scrambled eggs, hash browns, sausage links, bacon, pancakes, oatmeal, fruit salad, and cereal. A lot of people didn't know this, but I loved The Citadel's food. Those women work their asses off in the mess hall. I think they deserve more love and appreciation for what they do. I don't know many places that can feed over 2,500 people at one time, three times a day. I made a point to say thank you to them every day.

After breakfast we convened once again for another hour to go over plays that we needed to work on based on Thursday's practice and what we had seen of the other team. Coach Drayton and Coach Houston led the meetings for the defensive side while Coach Thompson led the meetings for the offensive side. These meeting were followed by a walk-through, which is the most important part of game day preparation. It is the mental preparation. As a team we must all be mentally prepared for what to expect. It's the last time for our minds to prepare for what plays we might see from our opponent. However, most importantly, it gives the coaches reassurance that we know what to do.

Mary's eyebrows knitted together. I could tell she was just about to ask me another question. "I bet you're wondering what exactly we do during a walkthrough, aren't you?" I asked her and she nodded.

"A walkthrough is a slow-motion mental and physical preparation that we as a team do to make sure everyone is all on the same page and ready come game time," I told her. "It's visualization of what to do in different situations against different plays. It helps with picking up on the other opponent's formations and, based off their formations, figuring out what plays are expected for them to run. "

"But why do they call it a walkthrough?"

I laughed. "That's a good question. In all honesty it should be called a runthrough, because it doesn't involve walking, but it's called that because it's not a practice but a mental preparation."

Walkthroughs are crucial to success on game day. Generally, nobody on the team messes up on walkthroughs, and that year was no exception. We'd had an entire week to prepare, and with it being the first game of the season, we'd had the entire summer to prepare for this game. Everybody on the team knew what to do. Coach always said, "If you don't know now, you better figure it out, because the hay is in the barn."

After walkthroughs, we went back to the hotel to hang out and relax for a couple hours. I always called this the calm before the storm. A lot of the coaches gave us packets: a player's quiz to fill out with play recognition, formation alignment, and assignments, along with different play calls.

"Oh wow!" Mary exclaimed. "You had to take a quiz? There are quizzes on football teams?"

"I know, right? As if I didn't get enough of that from our great institution's academia. But yes, the quizzes along with the walkthroughs helped us truly visualize what we were about to do as players. They helped us think what we needed to be thinking come game time."

The next part on the itinerary was the pregame devotion, followed by the pregame meal. Coach Frosty led the pregame devotion. As I said earlier, his ability to use scripture that molded the minds of young eighteen- to twenty-one-year-old football players was a gift. He had a tremendous ability to fire up the team through the Word. After every devotion, I was ready to go out and battle, not only for my team, but for my God, and to do all things through Christ who gave me strength.

The final part of our gameday plan was the final pregame meal. Since our game was at 4:00 p.m., our pre-game meal was at noon. (Coach liked to give us four hours to digest our food.) Once again, the menu was extensive, but I never liked to eat much before games. I think I am lighter and quicker on my feet if I haven't recently indulged. For that reason, I stuck to two bananas, a small portion of pasta, and a chicken breast.

"What's it like inside the mess hall? I mean, like, is it crazy? What's the environment like?"

"No, it's definitely not crazy. Quite the opposite, actually. It's quiet. Everyone has their headphones in and keeps to him or herself. Coach Houston hates when people are not focused and always liked to remind us that distractions before a game can ruin a team's success. All it takes is one player to throw off the entire dynamic of the team."

After the pregame meal, it was time to rock and roll. I went to Seignious Hall to get taped by the sport's medicine staff. Our helmets, uniforms and shoulder pads were already hanging in our lockers at the Altman Center at Johnson Hagood Memorial Stadium. Then, at around 3:50 p.m., we lined up as a team and headed to the buses wearing our travel suits, headphones, and, most importantly, our game faces. The bus ride was silent. Everyone was focused. I listened to my workout playlist on my iPhone.

We arrived at Johnson Hagood Memorial Stadium at 4:00 p.m. There were mountains of merchandise in Citadel blue piled up in front of the Altman Center and around the adjacent parking lots. The hype from last year all the way to this year had led to this moment. As I was walking off the bus I looked out at all the alumni, parents, and fans cheering us on. Out of all the thousands of Citadel fans, it was amazing that I could see the most important ones: my family. I got off the bus and walked toward my parents and Emily. "Joe, looking good, man," my father said as I approached. I had time to exchange a quick hug with each of them.

"Good luck, Joe."

"Go get it, Joe Cro."

"You got this, buddy. Play smart and within yourself."

All I could think about during that moment was the first kickoff—the key moment when we as a team would deliver the first punch to Davidson and set our precedent for the season.

As soon as we entered the Altman Center, we were met with a blast of cool air. It was one of those moments in which I really appreciate modern conveniences like air conditioning. Yeager and the equipment managers had placed everybody's helmets, shoulder pads, cleats, and uniforms neatly in our lockers. The outside linebackers' lockers were in the far back right of the room labeled "Kats and Bandits." My locker had my number on it with a piece of white tape: #5. Inside my locker was a game day brochure. Game day brochures contain information about the history of the school and summaries of the staff, the coaches, and the players.

I sat in my locker as I was getting into my game-day uniform. I put on my girdle first, followed by pants, socks and cleats. It was superstition for me that I always put on my left cleat first. Next, I went to Andy to get baby powder for my pants and more tape for my wrists and hands. I put on my half sleeves to cover up my forearms to my elbow.

"Wait, why do you wear only half a sleeve?"

"To cover up my elbow. After playing eight years on turf fields the layer of skin on my elbow is so thin that it will peel back anytime I slide on my forearms."

"Ouch that has to hurt!"

"Oh, it does. It's like a paper cut. More annoying and persistent than anything else."

I put on my entire uniform, minus the shoulder pads and helmet. I looked at Caleb, and we walked out onto the field together to warm up. I stretched and threw the ball with Caleb, as was our pregame tradition. One benefit of warmups was being able to see your opponent warm up as well. As we were throwing the ball, I sized up each individual player that walked by us from the other team, trying to intimidate them with my fierce gaze. It was a mental tactic, and it also helped me visualize taking one of them out come kickoff. I loved game day because it allowed me to take a step back and just focus on myself and football. That day I had extra time to loosen muscles that I normally would not have had time to stretch during the week. This extra time to prepare was crucial for my performance. The more flexible an athlete is, the quicker, faster, and stronger he or she will be. That's just fact. A loose muscle fiber is much more optimal for performance than a stiff one is. And that day I had to be completely loose.

After the warmup, Yeager called everyone back to the locker room to relax and to put on our helmet and shoulder pads and, most of all, to get pumped up. In the locker room, the atmosphere was serious. We were all focused. It was a nervous silence, with only music going in the background, as if we were in a C-17 Cargo plane getting ready to jump out to go to war.

"Have you done that before?"

"No. No, I haven't. But my Uncle Ed has, and he's told me some cool stories about it. He's an airborne ranger for the United States Army."

Finally, Coach D called out the first group to go on the field for more warmups. The order for warmups goes kickers, punters, returners, followed by quarterbacks, center, running backs, wide receivers and defensive backs, linebackers and fullbacks, and then offensive line and defensive line. The outside linebackers went with the third group. At about forty-five minutes till game time, Coach D called for the outside linebackers to line up and take the field. I got up out of my locker. Dondray and I, along with the rest of the squad, walked over to the doors, ready to take the field. My helmet was on and my adrenaline was at an all-time high. On our way out of the locker room I tapped a sign above the door that said *Play Like a Champion._*

Coach Weaver had us set up underneath the goal post for our warmups. There we lined up into two rows and did high knees and lunges. After we warmed up, he had us bang heads. This primarily was to get our bodies used to the physicality about to be unleashed come game time. After doing line tackling, he had us work on our stance, alignment, and first step. We did a drop back drill, working on our hips and footwork breaking to the ball. Then Coach Houston called for the defense to gather. Before each game the 1s and 2s on offense and defense lined up against each other to prepare us for the speed and physicality we were to expect come game time. I lined up with the 1s. On the defensive line from end-to-end it went Mark, Jon Jon, Mitch, and me. Behind me were James and Tevin at inside linebacker, Dondray at outside linebacker, Nick Willis and Diggy at safety, and Dee and Coop at cornerback. We ran six plays against the offense to get each other warmed up and prepared for the next four hours. After that, we punted the ball twice and kicked a field goal. It was almost game time!

Once the pregame ritual was over, we still had twenty minutes till kickoff. I ran to the end zone to join my teammates' huddle. James squeezed into the middle of us and started his famous chant, "Where my dawgs at?" We responded, "Wuff!" "Where my dawgs at?" "Wuff!" "Where my dawgs at?" "Wuff, wuff!" "Yeah, yeah, yeah!" "Beat Davidson's ass on three." "One, two, three… BEAT DAVIDSON'S ASS!!"

We jogged off the field into the locker room.

After downing a shot of test, a Powerade drink with extra electrolytes, I sat in my locker observing everyone. I saw the fire in their eyes. We were ready to set a precedent for the season. All we could think about was the coaches talking about how good Davidson was and how many returning All-Americans they had. It was our turn to prove to the world how many All-Americans we had on our team and to show Davidson what SoCon Football was all about. I took out a black sharpie pen and started to write on my wrist tape all of my whys.

"You've said that before," Mary said, "and I forgot to ask. What do you mean by your whys?"

"My 'whys' are my purpose for why I play the game and who I play it for."

"Oh, you mean whys like W-H-Y. I thought you meant Y like the letter."

"Well, it's no wonder you didn't understand, then," I said and we both smiled.

On my right wrist I wrote in big bold letters "GOD." For He was why I was able to play the game at this level and He had blessed me with everything that I had in my life. On my other wrist I wrote the initials TFL for Tucker Football League, which is where it all began. This was to remind me of former teammates and coaches that helped guide me along to where I was at that point. I remember back then Coach Marselas would always say, "All right, Joe, you are my captain." If it weren't for Coach Anthony Maddox, the head football coach of the hundred and twenty-pound lions getting me to come back and play football for him, I might not have ever played the game again and none of this would have ever come to fruition.

As I was reflecting more and more on my whys, I continued to write initials: SPX to represent the players and coaches from St. Pius X that helped develop me into the player I am today; people like Coach Jerry Stewart and Coach Paul Standard along with many of my former teammates; BC for Bubba Crochet, my uncle who passed away from cancer earlier in the year; NC, for Nelly Crochet, my grandmother who passed away the beginning of my knob year; UA, for Uncle Author; DC, for my father; EC, for my mother; DC, for my brother; EF, for my uncle Ed who has been a huge influence in my life and helped me be the man I am today. I wrote down a lot of my family members' initials. Lastly, I wrote TCF for The Citadel Football Program. I did this before every game to remind myself why I play the game and who I play it for. It was a constant reminder to think outside of myself during times of high adversity.

The game of football is much like the game of life, in that everyone is different. It takes all types to make the world go 'round. Having grown up in Tucker, Georgia, a middle-class suburb on the outskirts of town, I've been around all walks of life. From a young age, I've known that different things make different people tick. It's the same on a football team. Everyone gets pumped up differently. Coach D blares rap music to hype us up. Some guys, like Dondray and Shizz, wide receiver and punt returner, liked to dance before the game. Others like Sam and Kyle liked to just listen to their own music quietly. As for me, I liked to turn on my playlist and listen to "Not Afraid" by Eminem on repeat. It got me fired up because it put things in perspective. It reminded me that I was not afraid of anyone that stepped on this field to compete against me.

Twenty minutes later, Coach Houston called the team together in the locker room. "All right, guys… bring it up!" We responded by dropping to a knee to pray the "Our Father" and to ask God to watch over us on the field. Coach Houston gave his pregame speech. It was fiery. His face was red and spit started flying out of his mouth while he delivered the monologue that would serve as a prelude to a historic season.

"These guys don't respect you. They think they can come into our house and embarrass us on our field. Davidson can't disrespect us by showing up and playing on our field," he said. "I want them after the game to say to each other that they wish they had never driven down to Charleston, SC to play us." We all burst into a cheer. We were fired up. It was time to line up and take the field.

The crowd cheering was going crazy as we lined up to exit the locker room. The knobs were lined up on the field in the shape of a C and busy as beavers pumping up the crowd. As we exited the locker room we tapped the sign above the door—as if we needed a reminder. Austin Harrell, a three-hundred-pound defensive lineman, shouted: "Let's go!!!"

On the way to the end zone each of us touched the Joe Missar and Frank "Skip" Murphy statue before lining up in the end zone. Missar and Murphy, both from the class of '65, were two talented players who had given up their lives protecting our great country. It's a Citadel tradition for players to touch this statue before a game. It reminds us as players of a much greater reason for playing the game. We play for those who wore this uniform before us.

We gathered in the end zone behind Coach Houston. As soon as he got the go-ahead, we took off as a team, running through the alley of knobs to be welcomed by our supporters in Johnson Hagood Memorial Stadium. The crowd was going crazy. The game day captains selected by Coach Houston were already lined up on the fifty-yard line. The coin was flipped and The Citadel was going on defense first.

I remember lining up for that very kickoff—the first play of the game. I did my routine two high jumps, raising my legs to let the team know that I was ready to sprint down the field and unleash "Gretchen" on to them. Gretchen was the name of my grandmother's German shepherd. My uncle Edward Freeman, lieutenant colonel in the United States Army, would always play with her. Jokingly he would say that she was a crazy dog and had a look in her eye that she could kill anything that moves. She was the kind of dog that playfully and gently bit your forearm when you played with her. Sometimes, though, she would put her entire jaw around the wrist of whomever she was playing with so that his or her wrist would be in the dog's mouth. My uncle used to say she was feeling your heartbeat in your pulse on her canine teeth. She was letting you know that in the flip of an eye, she could end your life with one bite. Gretchen was a friendly dog, but she had a side to her that was beastly. I adopted the persona of Gretchen at a young age. Nice boy off the field, polite, with good manners; however, as soon as I strap up and put my helmet on… the beast was ready to be unleashed.

Gretchen was alive and ready to show the world what he could do. Eric Goins kicked the ball….

Showtime!!!!

"Champions aren't champions because they do anything extraordinary. Champions are champions because they do the ordinary better than anybody else."

- COACH CHUCK NOLL

Chapter 12:

WILL THE TWENTY-THREE-YEAR DROUGHT END?

First and ten Davidson. I looked at Mitch and Mark… it was show time. "Down, set, hike!" They snapped the ball and it was an inside zone run to the read side. (Wham!) Nick and James came out of nowhere and completely destroyed the kid. There was no room for him to go anywhere. Coach Houston yelled from the sidelines, "Let's go, defense. Get that ball back to us." All I could think about was delivering that first punch. Second and nine. "Set, hike!" The quarterback threw a dump pass to the wide out crossing in front of Tevin. (Wham!) Tevin rocked the poor defenseless receiver into next year. "Not today," Tevin said to the player, looking at him as he got up from the ground. Third down and seven yards to go for the first down.

Now for those that don't know the tradition of Citadel Football, third down is famously coined by our defense as the *money down*. It is the most important down in all of college football. If we stop the offense on third down, then it's very likely that they would punt the ball back to us—that is, unless we were within field goal range or a short

144

yardage situation.

Football is like a game of chess. It's all about field location and putting your team in the best position to score. The best defense is a great offense and the best offense—well, is a great defense. Special teams are very important, and don't get me wrong, I loved hanging out with the specialists; however, defense wins championships. As we lined up for the first third down of the season the announcer said, "Everyone stand up, for it is money down!" The sidelines were rocking; the fans were cheering, and we as a team were not going to let them get anywhere close to a first down. First punch…first punch… first punch!

"Set, hike!" It was a drop back pass. We only rushed three and I dropped back into coverage. The wide receiver sneaked behind James and the quarterback threw a nice pass into the curl. "Damnit, he got the first down." I had to remind myself, it was a marathon, not a sprint. All we could do was go out there and give it our best for the next three downs and try to force a punt or get a turnover. The season before, we hadn't done a very good job of creating turnovers, so Coach Drayton had made sure in the off season that turnovers became our sole focus. For this game, we had to have a shutout and force three turnovers. I just wanted an interception. I had not gotten one since high school, and even then, it was in a scrimmage.

"Set, hike!" The quarterback ran a draw for two yards. Trust me, nobody was going to outrun our defense. With me being the third slowest guy out there (in front of Jon Jon and Mitch), we had a team of just dudes. Being the only white starter on the defense, I held my own as far as speed goes. In high school I ran a forty-yard dash in 4.58 seconds, but ever since I gained forty pounds, my forty-yard had slowed to around 4.80 seconds. We had some great athletes. No way was a white quarterback from a private school about to outrun us. Davidson couldn't get a yard on the next two plays. Coaches hollered from the sidelines, "Punt team." I ran off the field. We as a defensive unit gathered on the benches, caught our breath, got some water in us, and listened to Coach Drayton or one of the other position coaches go over corrections we needed to make in order to be successful later on in the game.

"Good shit, guys. That's how you do it!" I was a very vocal person on game days. I'm sure it was annoying to some of my teammates, but pumping other people up pumps me up and keeps me alert for the next play.

"Damn Dondray, you almost got you one," Dee said with a smile, looking back into the stands. Dray smiled.

"I'm gonna get me one come the end of the night."

"Not if I don't beat you to it," Coop chimed in.

I was just smiling, taking it all in. Coach Tesh was racking out the D-line about not getting a sack and telling them secrets and moves to enable success at getting to the quarterback. I looked over at Mitch and I could see in his eyes that he was definitely going to get one or two that night. No doubt about it, our defense was doing work on Davidson. Other teams have a tough time playing the triple option because it is disciplined, assignment-sound football. In other words, old school. Every player must be assignment-sound in order for the team to be successful. One small error or one player not doing his assignment will result in a "Touchdown Bulldogs."

The key to having a successful season was having our offense on the field three times longer than our defense. "And another huge run by Vinny Miller," the voice of the announcer rang out. It was first and ten on the twenty-five-yard line. Davidson didn't stand a chance if we played the way that we had been all offseason and all summer long. Dom hiked the ball and rushed up the middle, "Touchdown Bulldogs!" The cannons in the back of the west end zone went off:

146

"Bam, Bam, Bam!" Everyone was out of their seats screaming and yelling at the top of their lungs. We had some dogs in the trenches making a path for Dom to swoop into the end zone. We were on the freaking boards! 7–0. The Citadel Bulldogs over Davidson.

The best part about having a triple option offense is knowing the amount of time that they kill to drive down the field and score. The name of the game is strategy and our team always had the advantage as long as we were ahead. Eric kicked the ball through the uprights flawlessly. Hunter, the long snapper, ran off the field. "How'd my snap look?" I looked at Hunter.

"Dude, it looked great."

"Five minutes and thirty seconds left in the first quarter and The Bulldogs are rockin' n rollin' in Johnson Hagood Memorial Stadium."

Davidson put on a nice little drive, passing the ball every single down. They were driving down the field slowly, but surely. It was first and ten on our forty-seven-yard line. "Set, hike!" The quarterback dropped back to pass, rolled to his right, and released the ball. While the ball was in the air, I turned to try and find the target he was throwing to, and "Oskie" Dee swooped in front of the wide receiver, getting the first turnover of the year. "Thatta boy," Coach Houston said to Dee as he jogged back to the sideline. We sat on the bench to get a quick water break. Well, that was one. We still needed two more turnovers to meet Coach's standards. As for me, I believe in not only meeting the expectation, but going above and beyond. The standard is the benchmark.

"C-I-T-A-D-E-L" was being chanted from the middle of the stadium. We were dominating on defensive and abusing them on offense. As I was watching our offense on the field, a loud, "Hey Davidson, y'all should really stick to basketball," emanated from somewhere in the crowd. It sounded like it came from the section of the Corps. "You should stick to basketball. Football is not your sport," another cadet yelled at a Davidson player as he lined up for kick off. I'm all for team spirit, but trash-talking is not something I find appealing. I'm the kind of person that lets my play do the talking. I stay away from belittling my opponents, because I respect the commitment they have decided to take to be a student-athlete at a Division I school. Even though we're on other teams, we both know the feeling of being ridiculed and judged by people that do not understand or comprehend what it takes to be wearing our jerseys. I cannot support trash talking; however, I love our student section.

Inky Johnson, former cornerback for Tennessee and former Tucker Lion, put it best: He believed that true fans are called supporters because they pay money to support our sport to watch the game. I totally agree with him and I think most of the people in the stadium are supporters; however, throughout my short career at The Citadel I have seen bandwagoners, "fans," and everything else under the sun other than supporters. My dream—my team's dream—was to one day have nothing but supporters in our stands cheering us on. We knew that the only way to do that was to win ball games, and right now we had to go 1-0.

It was first and ten on Davidson's twenty-yard line. Eric had a huge boot into the end zone, forcing a touchback. "Down, set…." We shifted as a defensive line to mess with the quarterback, "Hike!" We rushed four. Mitch and I bull rushed the offensive lineman, forcing the quarterback to make a quick pass. "Oskie" Tevin jumped in front of the Davidson wide receiver and took it back to the house. We chased him down to congratulate him in the end zone, but he was on cloud nine, not letting any of us catch up to him.

"And folks, that completes the first quarter."

We took a quick TV timeout before lining up to go back on defense.

That was turnover number two for Coach Drayton. All we needed was one more, and we would be in great shape. The crowd was going crazy. We scored the next drive. It was 28-0 and not even the end of the second quarter. We just couldn't take our foot off the gas.

And that's what we did… pedal to the metal. We kept punishing Davidson on offense and defense for two more quarters. We even let our second and third string play most of the fourth quarter. In the end, we beat Davidson 69-0. It was a defensive shutout and an almost perfect offensive display. The announcer summed it up nicely: "Dom ran for two touchdowns, passed for a third, and the fullback ran for three. The defense had four interceptions. Tevin returned an interception twenty-eight yards for a score, Dondray Copeland's interception set up Dom's seventeen-yard touchdown strike to Jorian Jordan, and Mariel Cooper's pick led to Dom's one-yard touchdown run."

After the game was when the real fun began. We partied like rock stars that night. For it being the first game of the year—our "statement" game—and being able to put a shutout as well as score almost seventy points put a target on our backs early. We had set a precedent. The country would know that we were not the same team as the previous year. Beating Davidson was a great win. Any time a team at our level pitches a complete shutout and scores sixty-nine points, it is quite an accomplishment. This game put us on the map and set us apart from many of the other teams in the country.

The preseason conference ranking had placed The Citadel in second-to-last place in the SoCon and one hundred and fifteenth in the country. The coaches of other teams in the conference did not respect our program nor did the local and national media predict that we would be a good team that year. (No surprise there: The media has always been for other schools and, in all fairness, we hadn't had a conference-dominating program since 1992.) Bottomline: we'd have no respect from anyone until we won a Southern Conference championship. Knowing this motivated us to perform and play at our very best every Saturday. After getting out all of the nervous jitters in the first game we could focus on preparing for the next. We were just going to have to show the rest of the world one game at a time.

Our next game was scheduled for September 12, another home game, this time against Western Carolina, who had placed second in the preseason rankings. They had over twenty returning starters and a veteran quarterback leading the team. Historically, Western Carolina had never been good at stopping our offense, but defensively we had not done a great job stopping theirs either; It was like watching Baylor play TCU, a matchup of offense versus offense. We all knew the game was going to come down to who can stop the other team's offense more times and who can capitalize on turnovers, third downs, and big plays.

The first quarter we played them well. We had a clear homefield advantage, especially because Cullowhee, North Carolina is up in the mountains where the air is dryer and cooler than it is in Charleston. In fact, temperatures in Cullowhee during that week had never reached above eighty degrees. Down in the Lowcountry, however, we had been practicing in temperatures of over ninety degrees. Furthermore, we had spent the summer installing a defensive package to stop the run-pass-option offense that Western was most known for.

Fortunately, our hard work and preparation paid off.

"Dom rushed for two touchdowns, Mitchell moved into fifth on The Citadel's all-time career sacks list with 1.0 sack, and Dee Delaney had two interceptions."

We took over the conference beating Western. This victory put us in first place in the conference, making us 1-0 in conference play and letting the rest of the conference know that we were here for the title. The next day's headline read: "Western Carolina is subjugated by The

Citadel 28 -10."

So, that was two knockout fights for us. We had started the season off strong, 2 - 0 and 1 - 0 in the SoCon. All we had to do was keep the ball rolling.

"The game of life is a lot like football. You have to tackle your problems, block your fears, and score your points when you get the opportunity."

-LEWIS GRIZZARD

Chapter 13:

A Dog Loves to Go on Road Trips

Our next game was against Georgia Southern, also known as the party school of the South. I actually loved away games. I enjoyed playing at other stadiums in different environments, but my favorite thing about away games was bonding with my teammates on the bus journey. Although the rides were sometimes long, they provided a chance for the team members to bond. And we made sure the journeys were fun. We did everything from listening to music, talking about sports, and watching movies to debating the next move for the party scene coming up. Another popular road-trip activity was to download Tinder and see who could get the most matches—an activity in which I did not partake. As you know, I was already seeing Emily; and besides, the thought of having so much temptation on my phone really rubbed me the wrong way. My teammates got a kick out of it, though, especially the defensive backs, who tended to receive the most matches. They were the pretty boys of the team.

In addition to enjoying the camaraderie on board, I also appreciated the opportunity to see more of the country. Before enrolling at The Citadel, I hadn't seen much—only Georgia, South Carolina, Florida and Colorado, which is less than eight percent of the United States. That changed quickly and by the time I was a junior, I was becoming a seasoned road-tripper. Life on the road is tough, but when you're with the right people, it's a lot of fun.

When it came to seating on the bus, you had to earn your stripes. Only the veterans of the travel team or people in the two deep were able to claim a seat. The starters had first option and didn't have to share a row. This being my second season as a starter, I always liked sitting toward the back of the bus near the bathroom so I wouldn't have to go through a labyrinth of bodies every time I had to pee. One rule everyone followed… no pooping on the bus. All of the starters on the defense agreed with me on this matter: I sat in front of Mitchell, behind James Riley, and to the right of Mark Thomas. This seating arrangement also provided privacy in our conversation so that a coach or alumnus would not be able to screen our conversations. (Not that we were saying anything bad—just having guy talk.)

We took lot of great bus trips, but my favorite would be either traveling to Clemson, SC, because it was a short bus trip and I love the Clemson Memorial stadium, or traveling to Cullowhee, NC, a journey which took us through the mountains during the peak of fall foliage season. On that trip we also got to stay at a beautiful and peaceful mountain golf resort.

Georgia Southern was a tough environment to play in. Not only were they a Sunbelt Conference team, but they ran the triple option, leaving our team with little advantage. We knew going into the game that it was going to be tough. They were more athletic, bigger, and they knew how to stop our offense. They kicked our butt the entire game. Offensively we went three and out almost every time, and defensively we played the worst game we had ever played in our lives. It was an all-around disaster. When third quarter rolled around, our offense was stopped for another three and out. We had to punt the ball. Ken Allen, Tevin Floyd, and I were on the punt shield, protecting the punter. Hunter Morris snapped the ball. All of a sudden, number eighteen from Georgia Southern came untouched through the line of scrimmage with a ten-yard full-speed start right at me. I was thinking to myself as I saw this mammoth of a guy coming full steam ahead at me, "Great, the biggest guy on Georgia Southern leaked through. This is fixing to hurt."

My dad taught me at a young age that in football you are either the hammer or the nail. As a linebacker, it is imperative to be a hammer; however, in this very instance I was left out to dry. My helmet had nail written all over it. It was not fun being a blocking dummy, all alone, while a two-hundred-and-fifty-pound hammer was brought to stuff me. I started reviewing my options quickly: the first option was to get in front of the guy and take it like a man; the second option was to let him free, in which case he would block the kick. As he continued toward me I remembered Coach Houston talking about us being a family. I couldn't let my brothers down. I decided to take it head on, putting the left side of my facemask on the player. (BAM!)

I immediately started seeing stars. He had knocked me into a new century. Everything went black. Apparently, after we collided, I fell straight backward and tried getting up but kept falling. I blacked out for a couple of seconds. I felt a stinging sensation down my arm and my spine. I felt nauseous and dizzy. Could I have really just gotten knocked out by that guy? Andy rushed over to check on me. Coach Weaver took one look at me and said "Shit." Andy pointed his flashlight toward my eyes and kept asking me questions. I don't remember what he said or what I said in response. All I could think about was the pain in my head and neck from that experience. Eventually I was able to get up and make my way, slowly, back to the bench to sit down. Unfortunately, it was true—I had suffered a concussion. And, we had ended up getting crushed 48-13. A huge defeat and a disappointing momentum switch. Instead of being 3-0 we were now 2-1. To make matters worse, I didn't even know if I was going to be able to play in the next game against our intra-city rivals, Charleston Southern University.

"There are more important things in life than winning or losing a game; However, if we look at life as a game, we play it to win."

- JOE CROCHET

Chapter 14:

CONCUSSIONS... OR "AW HELL, YOU'RE FINE"

We got home late that night. My head was throbbing relentlessly. The next day, Andy sent me home to recover and told me to stay in my room all day, to sleep and drink plenty of water. I missed Sunday's workout and practice and for the rest of the week I was supposed to remain "non-contact" in practice. (A nearly impossible order to follow in college football). For the next week I felt dazed and out of it, cloudy. I had trouble focusing.

The NCAA-concussion protocol is a joke. You could even argue that it's non-existent. No matter how bad a player feels or how hurt he is, there is no form of measuring traumatic injury. It's sad that a movie had to bring the severe issue of concussions and the implications of chronic traumatic encephalopathy (CTE) to light before the NCAA and NFL would even speak up on the matter. Concussions have tremendous neurological impact on the players, and I am horrified to see what they have done to my body throughout my entire sixteen-year career. Though I was taught to toughen up and suck it up, I wish I had known the impacts being tough would have on me later in life. I might not have been so quick to get back out there on the field.

I find it very curious that the NCAA is a nonprofit organization, yet, they can make billions of dollars in revenue each year exploiting athletes. The worst part about it is they profit at the expense of the athletes' health. The athletes are the one sacrificing and putting their lives in jeopardy, and for what? The almighty dollar and some entertainment. My biggest issue with the NCAA is that they have these rules and regulations, but they fail to enforce the most important one—the one that protects the athletes and looks out for their overall health. It seems to me they should feel some form of responsibility when a serious injury occurs. But they don't.

The NCAA and NFL have knowingly withheld a lot of the information about the severity of these injuries, and I promise to God I will not do the same. Instead, I am going to do everything in my power to make sure that kids in college and high school learn about the huge commitment they are making if they decide to play football. The scariest statistic I have ever read was the recent finding based on CTE scans of two hundred and two deceased NFL players: ninety-nine percent of them tested positive for the degenerative brain disease. There have also been reports of it being found in college football players after they have passed from either suicide or accidental death.

Money is a form of power; however, money without knowledge will not get you far in life. If you don't get anything out of this book other than me educating you about the severe risks of concussions and CTE, then I will have achieved my goal, because you will at least have that knowledge. Someone needs to call out the NFL and NCAA for their negligence and information- laundering. We as athletes put ourselves at risks much greater than we ever thought, and for what? To win football games? To get an education? For some, it's a price they're willing to pay; however, I ask the person looking in the mirror to think twice about whether it is worth sacrificing much more than just four years of your life in order to attain a piece of paper and win football games. If you're up for it, then rock on, brother. Don't get me wrong, I love the game of football. I loved the life lessons I have attained from it. I loved the locker room atmosphere and the brotherhood it cultivated. I loved being able to represent something much greater than just myself. I loved being able to say I was a Division I football player. I loved that I was able to make my family and friends proud of me. I loved that I was able to travel to places I would otherwise never have been, and to meet some of the greatest people I would ever meet. There are way more positives than negatives with the game of football; however, I do not like the way athletes are largely exploited by institutions and deemed expendable the moment they get hurt. Looking back, I seriously question whether or not the concussions and possible side effects of CTE were worth it.

On another note, the only way I could go to school out of state was by being on a football scholarship. Playing for The Citadel was and still is the best four and a half years of my life. The brothers I made as well as the experiences I shared with them will be something I will cherish forever. I'm not trying to take anything away from the great game of football; I am just bringing awareness of the true risks that are involved and pointing out a corruption that needs to be addressed. My issue does not lie with the coaches or staff members of any college program; it lies with the people on the boards and committees of these large bureaucracies that make way more than they deserve but do not take care of their athletes who sign to play in their organization.

Football is a great game, but it can take a tremendous toll on your body. Like many former athletes, I deal with this every day. I suffer from complications of anxiety and many of my doctors believe it is from the traumatic injuries I sustained throughout my football career. It could be CTE, or it could be that a part of my brain has been severely traumatized over the years. Either way, I now have to deal with that.

As much as I hate to say it, I am a victim of the NCAA.

Coaches are not doctors, and neither are the sports athletic trainers. There needs to be an actual team doctor—one who is paid for by the NCAA and NFL--who is up to date on this subject, to diagnose, treat, and make the judgement call on whether or not a player has a concussion, can play, or needs to sit out more to really allow his body time to heal. Concussions are the number one injury in college football.

The NCAA and the NFL need to own up to their negligence and stop pretending that the game we play is all fine and dandy. They are the true criminals letting kids at young ages mindlessly play a game without exposing the truth behind what really can happen. It is troubling that they say, "Oh well, that kid decided to play; it's ultimately his decision. We aren't responsible for him even though we know later in life he might have complications if he doesn't learn about the true risks and ways to play the game safely."

Anyway, where was I? Oh, right—by Wednesday my condition had improved somewhat, so I asked Andy if I could play that weekend. Medically, I probably should have given myself a lot more time to fully recover, but I couldn't let my team down... right? They were counting on me...I had to play. This is a very common situation for athletes throughout college, the NFL, and even high school. The pressure from family, friends, and coaches can cloud your judgment and get in the way of making an objective decision. Playing injured is one thing, but playing with unknown consequences—well, that's something I wish I had known more about.

As I was sitting by my locker thinking, reflecting, drifting, Coach Houston walked in.

"Joe, how you feeling?"

I smiled up at him. "I'll be ready to go come Saturday!"

"That's what I like to hear; need a good practice out of you today. Our team is counting on you."

"Do you know what my favorite part of the game is? The opportunity to play."

- MIKE SINGLETARY

Chapter 15:

CAN THE CURSE OF
1992 BE.... LIFTED?

O ur game against Charleston Southern was to be our last night game of the season, with kickoff scheduled for 6:00 p.m. We owed CSU a can of whoop-ass after the last game they played against us. Historically, The Citadel has always beaten CSU. Normally, it wasn't even a competitive game, and they still played in a high school stadium. However, ever since Jamey Chadwell became their head coach in 2012, their program had undergone a transformation. They went from being a below-average FCS football team to being a top-twenty-five program overnight. I gave credit to the players and the new coaching staff.

There was not a team more despised in the eyes of Coach Houston than CSU. Apparently, he and Coach Chadwell had quite a long history coaching against each other, dating back to their college-playing years. Both coaches' passion to beat the other was more than evident. It was like sibling rivalry, determining which one was the alpha male. That's the kind of close-knit rivalry that brings the hardest battles.

I was nervous—not because we were playing CSU, but because the game would be the first time I'd be engaging in live physical contact since suffering my concussion. Thinking about the game, I asked myself what was the worst that could happen.

Charleston Southern won the toss and elected to kick. We lined up to receive the ball. It soared way over Quinlan Washington's head. Touchback, first and ten, Bulldogs from the twenty-five-yard line. Dom got behind center: "Down, set, hike!" He dropped back and threw a screaming pass to Vinny Miller that went barely over his head. Second and ten, "Down, set... check, check." Dom checked because Charleston Sothern's defense was moving and gave him a different pre-snap read. "Set, hike!" Evan McField got the handoff for a short yardage gain. Third and long for the Bulldogs.

I was on the sideline with my helmet on, ready to go. The previous year, Charleston Southern had gotten away with barely beating us and we were not going to let it happen again this year. "Set, hike!" Cam motioned right in the backfield as they ran a quarterback power to the right. Dom rushed for about six yards before getting tackled short. We elected to punt. Will Vanvick got the snap from Hunter. It was a high punt. We downed it at the CSU thirty-nine-yard line. First and ten Buccaneers.

We, as a defense, were fired up. Coming off our embarrassing loss against Georgia Southern just made us want to go out there and prove that that had been an anomaly. We needed to let the people know who we were and what Citadel football was all about. Now was our chance. We could not let ourselves be remembered by that last embarrassing loss. So, we were a team that gave up forty-four points to GSU. Well, that was then and this was now. Now was tonight when we beat CSU! It was time for redemption!

CSU was in a pistol formation. CSU broke the huddle; we aligned in our defensive set. Mitch lined up in the three-technique next to me; Tevin was lined up in the A-gap on my side and I was in a five-technique outside of the offensive tackle. More than likely from watching film and understanding formation alignment, CSU was going to do an inside zone to the left or going to do an RPO (run-pass option) play hitting the wideout on the other side.

"Down, set!" The starting quarterback for CSU was a transfer from University of Alabama at Birmingham (UAB) and supposedly a top tier quarterback in FCS. (Well, at least according to the media.) "Hike!" They snapped the ball. It was an inside zone to the left side. The running back got two yards before being met by Tevin, Mark, and Mitchel. Second and eight for the Buccaneers. They lined up again in a pistol formation. Two backs to left and right side behind the quarterback with an H back, tight end, in motion behind the offensive tackle. The tight end was more than likely there to block. "Down, set, check, check!" as he and the rest of the team looked to the side lines. "Run the play, run the play," called the CSU offensive coach. "Hike!" It was another inside run to the other side. I was getting very eager. I just wanted them to run my way so I could get my first tackle in. We as a team had delivered our first punch to CSU, but as a player just coming back from a concussion, I still had to deliver mine.

"Hike!" CSU threw an eight-yard pass. First down Bucs. "Hike!" The quarterback sprinted my way on a sprint out pass play. I ran to try to get to him before he released the ball, but I was too late. The quarterback threw the ball just barely over my fingertips to complete the pass for a six-yard gain. Second down and four: "Down, set, hike!" The running back jumped. Yellow flags bombarded the field like World War II dropping bombs on Germany. "False start on the offense, that will be a five-yard penalty, replay second down." It was second and nine now for the Bucs. My anxiousness was overwhelming me. They had yet to run the ball to my side. I needed to get this tackle in. I needed to make a play. After all I wanted to be an All-Conference Outside Linebacker, and without stats I was not going to get there. "Set, hike!" The offensive tackle dropped back as if it were a pass. Immediately I realized it was a quarterback draw. The quarterback pretended to drop back for a pass and then took off up the middle. It was like a shark sensing blood in the water (and I was the shark). The quarterback didn't even see me coming. As he cut right, Bam! I delivered all two hundred forty-five pounds of my body weight along with all of the force in my body into him. I led with the right side of my helmet and shoulder pad into his upper torso. Bam! A loud hit. The quarterback fell immediately to the ground, but his helmet went flying ten yards behind him. "Ooooh" and loud cheering came from our cadet section. I had knocked the crap out of him.

"'Bout time you got that first hit back in. I've been waiting on you, Joe, to make a play." Mitch smiled at me as we lined up for third down.

"I'm back, brother," I said to Mitch with a laugh. That one clean hit had felt like hitting a cloud. It had released from my body all the built-up adrenaline, stress, anger, and other emotions I'd been carrying since my concussion. I felt more focused now, and my nerves were calmed. I had regained confidence in my ability to "lay the wood." Incidentally, it is an NCAA rule that if a player's helmet comes off as a result of a play, he must sit out for at least one play until returning to the game.

The rest of the first half we played lights out. We ended up scoring two touchdowns and a field goal and only gave up a touchdown (blocking their extra point, at least). Dom hurdled two CSU defensive players to score our first touchdown; Eric knocked down a forty-yard kick, and Dee got an interception and returned it back to the house. We were playing like a championship football team. We just needed to clean up on a couple of the mistakes and this game was ours. Dondray also had an interception in the first quarter that sparked our touch-down drive. We went into half-time 17-6. As long as we kept up this momentum, we had it.

Now remember that I told you the most important part of this game was the start? Well, I was wrong. Actually, there are two keys to being successful in this game. Start and finish. The alpha and omega. The successful start put us in a great spot as a team; however, if we screwed up and let them score two touchdowns, then we would lose the game. No! We had to finish stronger than we started.

We came back from half-time to get a quick stretch with Coach D. Then it was back to the game. We kicked the ball off and ended up going back and forth the rest of the night. You know that feeling when you very much want something to happen but no matter how hard you try, your efforts keep falling short or even backfire on you? Well, sadly, that was what happened to us. We shat a brick. Defensively we gave up too many yards and offensively they shut us down. We ended up losing the game to CSU 33-20.

It did not feel great losing that game. It was a game we should have won. To make matters worse, after the game Coach Chadwell and his players stormed the field with brooms and took off their shoulder pads revealing an undershirt with the words "Sweep The Citadel" in big bold letters. Now, according to every book I've ever read about human nature, a person's true character can be measured by how he or she handles him or herself at his or her lowest moments; however, I believe the opposite. I believe a person truly reveals his or her true self at their highest moments. The highest moments are the times when people have a choice to be humble or to be arrogant jackasses. CSU and that coaching staff were not humble. We were 2-2 for the season and 1-0 in the SoCon.

My mentality every time I stepped on that field was to win. I played the game to win. In the grand scheme of things, however, these two losses would not prevent us from achieving our goal of winning the conference championship. We had played only one conference game, making us 1-0 in the SoCon. The dream was still alive as long as we learned from these two losses. We had to grow and play our best football, improving in every subsequent game. Reality sank in: Every game mattered from here on out.

Our next matchup would be against Wofford. The previous year we had lost to Wofford in Spartanburg, South Carolina on a blown call. It was fourth and one from the goal line with one second left on the play clock. Aaron Miller dove into the end zone to score; however, the referee said that he was down before entering the end zone. We lost that game because the SoCon did not have instant replay for the referees to watch, and therefore teams could not challenge the call. I was furious and upset, along with everyone on our team. The jumbotron in the back-end zone even showed the replay, but the call could not be reversed. I was so upset. I remember going back onto the bus and cussing up a storm. I said some things I regret saying about my Lord and Savior Jesus Christ. Mitchell and Mark had to calm me down in the back of that bus. I couldn't sleep or do anything for a couple of days.

The reason why this game was such an emotional game and there was so much passion behind it is because The Citadel had not beaten Wofford since September 12, 1998. It had been seventeen years since The Citadel beat Wofford. That was seventeen years of getting our ass torn by one head coach and by one program. To top it all off, their mascot was a terrier. What the heck is a terrier, anyway?!

To rub it in our faces even more, Wofford had come up with a "Big Dog Trophy" to acknowledge the winner of this matchup each year. It was very similar to the Shako trophy that was given out to the winner of the Military Classic Bowl between The Citadel and VMI. Having not beaten Wofford in seventeen years, many of us were unaware of the Big Dog Trophy's existence.

Well, we may not have known about the trophy, but we did know that we had to end our losing streak. We well remembered our loss from the year before. We were more fired up than ever. "Payback is a bitch," was our mantra when it came to playing Wofford. After taking two embarrassing losses and the recent memory of last year in Spartanburg, we really felt it was our turn to take charge and show the conference that we meant business. From the first play of the game, the little Terriers would not want anything to do with us. We had just gone through one of the hardest weeks of practice going "live" every day with the starting offense versus the first team defense in scrimmage.

If Wofford thought they were going to just show up and dominate us like they had in the past, they would be very mistaken. From the first punch we hit them so hard they didn't know what to do. Our defense played lights out. Their quarterback was too afraid to even hike the ball. Offensively, we ran all over them. It was a one-sided game the entire time. We beat Wofford 39-12. The drought against Wofford was over! The Citadel finally beat Wofford for the first time in seventeen years. It was a great feeling—not only winning, but winning so impressively. We were beginning to rewrite history.

We were now 3-2 and 2-0 in the SoCon. Our next game would be away at Samford in Birmingham, Alabama. Traditionally, Samford was known for their "ginormous" players and talented defensive backs. In the last five years they had had four of their players drafted into the NFL and many others picked up as free agents who are still currently playing in the league. I had a chip on my shoulder toward Samford. They recruited me in high school, but like many other schools, they thought I was too small to play for them. Well, now at six foot two and two hundred forty-five pounds, I think they might have underestimated me. Regardless, it was motivation for kicking their ass this next game.

We played Samford tough. Our fullback ran for three touchdowns, Dom ran for another, Vinny had a touchdown, Mark had a strip sack which Dee took back for a touchdown. Our defense played really inspired and focused, resulting in forcing four three and outs and four turnovers. I even jumped on a loose ball. Handily, we beat Samford 44-25. This game put us 4-2 for the season, 3-0 in the SoCon. We were on a great roll and the trip back, although one of longest of the year, was great.

Our next game was against our historic rival: the Furman University Paladins football team. They used to be called the Furman University Christian Knights until someone smart figured out that the acronym is deemed inappropriate for a Christian institution. Anyway, as most of you know purple makes any Citadel man puke, and there is a great reason for that. The Citadel versus Furman Football rivalry has had a rich history that dates back to 1913. As of 2017, there has been a total of ninety-seven meetings. Furman leads the series 59-35; however, The Citadel had the largest victory in the series where we won 75-0 way back in 1913.

Furman University was only three hours away and as an in-state rival, The Citadel-Furman game was similar to Clemson versus South Carolina. When we lost to Furman during my red-shirt freshman year I had made a promise to myself that that loss would be the only time I lost to that program.

Now don't get me wrong; I have nothing against Furman as an academic institution. When it came down to deciding where I was going to play college ball, it was between The Citadel and Furman. I enjoyed meeting their coaching staff and enjoyed learning about the school. However, it was an inner calling that told me to choose The Citadel. The Citadel chose me and, boy, am I glad I accepted the challenge.

We played up to our potential that day and beat Furman 38-17. I had my first career sack; Dom and Cam Jackson both rushed for two touchdowns. If it had not been for our offensive line, our running backs and quarterbacks would not have gotten anywhere that game. Our O-line are some dudes! Those five guys played every snap of the game. I give credit to Coach Boyd. He is one of the toughest guys I know and he breeds tough O-linemen. Any college football player who is able to play every down going against three hundred-pound-plus men every play is quite impressive, especially for a no-huddle triple option team. I would like to see Georgia Tech's O-line do what our guys can do.

Anyway, back to the story. With all the highs of winning I almost forgot to mention... I got another freaking concussion! Yep, another one... as I was tackling the running back at the same time one of our players was getting ready to unload... we collided. It was "friendly fire." My helmet took the complete force of James' knockout hit. He knocked me out of the game. Immediately I blacked out and passed out for a couple of seconds on the field. I had to go to the sideline, where I was later diagnosed with a concussion and had to miss the rest of the game. I thought, *Great, not only is this my last time playing at Furman, but I have to deal with having another concussion.*

(Remember what I said earlier in the book about being mindful of the risks of playing this game? The risks are real. Do not let your hubris prevent you from weighing all of the options before signing up for this collegiate sport. Your long-term health is more important than some win that will soon be forgotten. I suggest that every athlete become well-informed, be smart, and learn the facts. I'm an advocate and a football fanatic; however, I did not fully understand the seriousness involved until late in my career. CTE is a very real medical problem resulting from repetitive physical trauma, such as helmet-to-helmet collisions. Much more research needs to be done to improve safety of the sport.)

The next week was Homecoming—the time of year when cadets' family members and Citadel alumni arrive on campus. It was such a special time and drew the largest crowd of the season to Johnson Hagood Memorial Stadium, making it the perfect opportunity to broadcast your talent to Citadel supporters. I felt great going into Homecoming weekend. I'd been undefeated in all of the Homecoming games in which I had ever played, and that's going all the way back to second grade. Sixteen years of undefeated Homecoming games! There was no way I was going to break tradition now. That year we'd be playing Mercer. Kick-off was at 2:00 p.m.

"Do you know what the most important two games of the year are for a senior?" I asked my seat companion. She looked at me, confused.

"Ummm... no, I don't. Can you tell me?"

"Homecoming and something called Senior Day, which is the last home game of the season. These two games are what seniors remember most in their last season, and I—along with everyone else—wanted to send out my classmates with wins in both games."

It was Halloween in Charleston, South Carolina. The temperature was a perfect 75 degrees and sunny. The entire Johnson Hagood Memorial Stadium was packed out with only standing room on The Citadel home side. We played our butts off. The first quarter, Mercer went up 10-0. We scored fourteen points the second quarter. The third quarter was a defensive battle. I had one sack and a tackle for loss. Mitchell and Mark both took over defensively and put pressure on the quarterback. There was 12:51 left in the game. We killed the clock, running five minutes of it. Dom rushed for a three-yard touchdown and Eric made the extra point. We were up 21-13 with seven minutes and forty-nine seconds left in the game. Mercer answered and put on a seventy-five-yard drive for a touchdown to pull within two points. All I could think was: *Crap, we can't lose on Homecoming.* There was just three minutes and twelve seconds left in the game when Mercer lined up to go for the two-point conversion. "Down, set, hike!" The quarterback got the ball and tried to squeeze in to one of his receivers, but our defense did a great job applying pressure, forcing the quarterback to miss his mark. The ball fell to the ground. We won a really hard-fought game, 21-19. I was stilled undefeated on Homecoming!

Our next game was against VMI. Senior Day—the last home game of the season. It was a very emotional day for our team. This day marked the last day that I would ever play in Johnson Hagood Memorial Stadium with some of my classmates—my brothers and closest friends. After today, all the great times of the last four seasons would be relegated to the record books as memories. Who was going to tell our story? That's what I kept thinking during one of the most important games of my life. Not only was it Senior Day, but we were undefeated in the Southern Conference. We were number one. All we had to do was beat VMI and then we would be automatic Conference Champions. (Well, as long as Chattanooga lost; Chattanooga was playing Mercer—one of the best teams in the league. They had lost every game by a touchdown or less.)

Senior day, conference championship title, and oh yeah, I almost forgot to mention… we were competing for the Silver Shako trophy.

"Remember the Silver Shako trophy I mentioned before?" I asked Mary who, I was happy to see, was still paying attention.

"From the military teams?" she replied.

"That's right. The military institutes. The Citadel versus VMI game, also known as the Military Classic Bowl. The trophy is handed off to the winner. It's kind of like the Army versus the Navy game, but at the FCS level."

174

"I get it," said Mary, nodding. "Go on with your story. Did you win?"

It was quite a special moment. All of our seniors lined up and walked onto the field with their respective loved ones at the beginning of the game. Kyle, James, Sam, and I were captains—as were all of the seniors from the class of 2016. Not many understand the impact this class had made on The Citadel, especially on The Citadel football program. We were pioneers for generations to follow. All we had to do was beat VMI, and we would seal history.

And, let me tell you, we dominated that game, playing as if we had just come of off a huge loss, as if we were angry. Many people might fold under pressure or play the game not to lose. That was not our mentality. Our mentality was to thrive, not just survive. And thrive we did. We beat VMI 35-14. We passed the ball for one hundred thirty-four yards and rushed for three hundred twenty-six. Defensively, we held VMI to two hundred total yards. Q had two interceptions, with one being a ninety-one-yard touchdown return. Tevin had another interception which he returned for a seventy-five-yard touchdown and Malik, our safety, had an interception as well.

After the game while we were celebrating in the locker room, Tyus Carter yelled out, "Guys, Chattanooga is losing to Mercer!" We all stopped what we were doing and rushed over to Tyus's locker to watch the remainder of the game. My adrenaline was going crazy. It was like a scene from the movies. Not only did we beat VMI on Senior Day, claim the Silver Shako, and stay undefeated in the SoCon, but Chattanooga was about to lose. If Chattanooga lost, then we would clinch the Southern Conference as 2015 Conference Champs. This had not happened since 1992: twenty-three years of Citadel football without a conference championship win. Actually, there had only been two conference championship teams in the entire hundred-and-eleven-year history of football at The Citadel, and we were just moments away from being a part of history, adding ninety more names to the list of Citadel champions. As we watched, everyone was dead silent. After a win, that was extremely unusual. Ordinarily, we would have been celebrating; however, this moment was much greater than celebrating any win.

Mercer was up 17-14 with a minute left in the game. My old teammate from St. Pius, defensive back Alex Avant, had an interception. Chattanooga had the ball driving to score. The seconds kept ticking. "Man, Mercer is about to lose this one," one of my teammates yelled. All of a sudden, interception Mercer! Mercer just stopped Chattanooga, who had no more timeouts. It was game over. Mercer had won!

We'd done it! We had just made history by making it to the first Southern Conference championship game since 1992. The locker room went from dead silent to so loud that I couldn't hear myself think. The defensive backs started blasting music through our loud speakers. I hugged Big Weaves, Caleb, and Eric, along with many of the other guys. It was a very emotional time. I don't think there is any form of stimulant in the world that can produce the amazing high we were enjoying. It was a high on life that had come only two other times to The Citadel football program history—and buddy, did we embrace it. After we celebrated in the locker room, I still could not get over the fact that we were champions.

Kyle, Caleb, Hunter, and I joined our parents at Red's Bar and Grill to celebrate. Let me tell you, I do not get drunk often, but that was a night to celebrate. As Charlie Baker says, "We partied like rock stars." Nothing beats a cold drink, a lit cigar, great food, and being with friends and family underneath the Charleston moon on Shem Creek. I do not think there was a finer recipe than that. That was what I call living the life!

We were slated to play Chattanooga next at their place. We could win the conference with a win. But it was a tough game and basically, we just did not show up. The mentality we had against VMI was not there. We were playing not to lose instead of flying around to the ball and playing to win. It was evident. That morning we had a tremendous scare as well. One of our players had to go to the ER for an immediate surgery regarding his reproductive organs. Also, the morning of the game CNN news headlines showed a terrorist attack in France. I'm not saying that had anything to do with how we played, but it was just an all-around bad day, made even worse when we lost to Chattanooga, 31-23. Talk about an upsetting defeat! My good friend Philip Poole and his family, along with my cousin Elizabeth and Aunt Diane, as well as Emily and her family, all came by to show support. We could have finished the year as outright So-Con Champions. Instead, we finished up the conference season sharing the conference title with UT Chattanooga.

"What do Bulldogs do first play and every play after that? Hit 'em in the mouth!"

- CHARLIE BAKER
CLASS OF 1971

Chapter 16:

THE CITADEL'S CHARLIE BAKER

"Hit 'em in the mouth. Come on, Bulldogs. First play, last play, every play… Hit 'em in the mouth!" This chant came from the first row in Johnson Hagood Memorial Stadium. The man chanting was Charlie Baker, class of 1971. He was a former middle linebacker for The Citadel and a big-time supporter of The Citadel football program. He was at every home game in the first section of the stadium, cheering us on to whoop someone's ass that day. He always had his megaphone to help our fans get riled up come game time.

Charlie is the most dedicated Citadel Bulldog there is. Some may say he's a little on the wild side during games; however, though he curses up a storm and has a tough exterior, he is one of the most loyal people I know, and his character reflects the essence of what it means to be a true Citadel man. A straight shooter is what I call him, a no bullshit kind of guy, a quintessential Citadel man. Nobody on earth is more passionate about Citadel football than he is. Being on his football scholarship, I got to know him quite well personally. Where do I begin

179

to tell you about Charlie?

The first time I met Charlie Baker was during my freshman year at the fall scholarship banquet. He and his wife sat next to me, and there was instant chemistry between us. Let me give you some more background on Charlie. Charlie is a man who has given his time, talent, and dedication to this great institution. The Citadel was not such a popular place to be from back in the days when Charlie Baker first matriculated in 1967. The Vietnam War was going on, and everyone in Charleston thought cadets from The Citadel were war mongers. He told me one afternoon while we were talking on the phone, "Joe, we would have fights downtown all the time. The days back then were much different. I would tell the guys that we would chase girls till 11 at night, and if that didn't work out, then we would find us a fight." Charlie is a guy that does not put up with any crap, and if there was a fight involving any of his teammates, best believe he was helping them out. He is a guy I want on my side in a bar fight even to this day.

Charlie played back when East Carolina, West Virginia, William and Mary, and Davidson were in The Southern Conference. A lot of people don't know this, but the SoCon was the first football conference in the South. A lot of great teams from the ACC and SEC originated from the Southern Conference. The Citadel used to be an SEC school before the SEC was even around, back then when everything was Division I-A. Now there are two divisions, FBS Division I-A and FCS Division I-AA, that make up all of NCAA Division I football. However, back in those days before the ACC and SEC, The Citadel was a dominant force that nobody wanted to play.

"You know, Joe, back when everything was Division I... the freshmen, who normally are used as blocking dummies and scout team players for the varsity, played five junior varsity games a year. My freshman year, we played University of South Carolina, East Carolina University,

180

University of Georgia, Furman, and Georgia Military College. I remember one of my teammates asking another, 'Hey Capazoli, did they tell you this was a military school when they recruited you? Capazoli said, 'Hell no, they didn't.' Those two guys didn't come back after Thanksgiving either. Out of the sixty guys that matriculated from my class on the football team, only fourteen of them graduated senior year." When I asked him why so many of them had left, he told me they just couldn't handle the road less traveled.

It's an astonishing fact that not even thirty percent of Charlie's classmates graduated with him. "Joe, the coolest thing to ever happen to me at The Citadel was my senior year, when I was the middle linebacker. My junior year and the years before that, we ran a fifty-defense stacking two linebackers behind the five-man defensive front. However, senior year we moved into a 4-3 defense. I still lined up in the middle, but I was the only one. I called the huddle and my high school teammate Jimmy King was the starting safety. We both went to high school together at Needham Broughton High school. We started on the same field together at The Citadel and in 2004 were inducted into The Citadel Football Hall of Fame." That is no lackluster accomplishment. Being named into The Citadel Football Hall of Fame means you were one the best football players to ever play at The Citadel. I hope one day I can join that long list of strong alumni that have been able to distinguish themselves from the entire roster one play at a time.

I asked him about his life post-football. "I was traveling all over the United States for work. It was quite the experience, and I loved every second of it, but I moved back to Charleston in 1981. In 1983 I founded The Citadel Alumni Football Association, currently known as The Citadel Football Association (CFA). Originally it was meant to get my former teammates back together after all of those years. I wanted to have something that could get the guys back together and have alumni games to whoop up on our varsity to make them see how real football is played. The CFA was originally founded as a letterman's club but is now open to anyone who is willing to help The Citadel Football program."

The CFA has done so much for our football program. During my freshman year, our facilities were pretty subpar for a Division I football program, to say the least. There were Division III schools with better facilities than ours. I knew of high schools in Georgia that looked more like a college program than what we had. The hotel we stayed in was an inn that smelled like marijuana and had cockroaches crawling everywhere. Thanks to the large support from alumni and the CFA, we were able to upgrade a majority of our resources to Division I standards. Seignious Hall's facilities received a large chunk of money from The Citadel Football Association to renovate its outdated weight room, locker room, meeting rooms, and waiting area. It gave all the players confidence to have these resources. There is something about the mindset: if you are treated like a championship program, you will play like one. Thanks to the CFA, we were starting to get our swag.

The new and improved Seignious Hall helped change the entire culture. We now had the best facilities in the conference. The renovations, the new contract with Adidas, along with support for better nutrition for the athletes created a like-minded culture where everyone started to buy into the process. Not just any process, but the process of winning.

For those that do not know, our mascot is "Spike" the bulldog; however, did you know that Spike was the brainchild of Charlie Baker? Probably not, because he is a guy that does things not to get credit, but to help make The Citadel better. Spike is just one of Charlie's many creations. He launched Spike right around the same time he started The Citadel Alumni Football Association when he was working for an ad agency. "Joe, I grew tired of having the same logo and mascot as UGA, Yale, Samford, Georgetown, Gonzaga, Mississippi State, and other colleges across the country. So, I took matters into my own hands to make a difference." It was a change that has distinguished our program.

Charlie took his idea for a new logo of a bulldog wearing a shako with a spiked collar to an artist. "I want a ferocious bulldog that looks like it will kick your ass and does not look anything like any of the other college mascots, I told the designer." After a couple of renditions and long nights developing a concept, the Spike that we know today came to life. The artist's drawing nailed everything Charlie was looking for.

"In 1985, I took the final rendition of Spike to General Grimsley and the athletic director, Walter Nadzak, Jr. They both loved it and approved of it right there on the spot." It was that simple. All it took was one person who had the confidence and drive to make a difference to actually impact society.

Another great idea of Charlie's was that Spike could fit inside the C of The Citadel as a logo or they could be separate. "In 1986, I introduced Spike to Charleston and alumni. That day, let me tell you Joe, it was a blast buddy. We kicked it all off with the Washington Redskins Cheerleaders dancing for the celebration. And they knew how to grab a Citadel man's attention!"

"Why were the Washington Redskin Cheerleaders there?" I asked. Well, they were there because Charlie made it happen. He's just that kind of person—a doer.

I do not know what Charlie is more passionate about—his love for Citadel Football or his hatred for Furman. Any in-state rivalry game is a huge matchup, but there is not one as big as The Citadel vs Furman game. Charlie will tell you, "I don't like them. We lost to them the last game of my senior year season. It cost us the SoCon championship. It was a rainy game with puddles on the field. We had just stopped

Furman and forced them to punt the ball. The ball hit the puddle of water. Jeff ran sideways to try and get away from the ball, but the damn ball was chasing him. It hit him in the side of the leg on the five-yard line and Furman recovered it. They ended up punching it in the last minute of the game. I never lost to Furman until that game. I dislike Furman a lot!"

Just like Charlie I am sure many alumni have similar disdain toward our upstate counterpart.

"So where is Charlie now? Does he still go to the games?" Mary asked.

"Nowadays you can find Charlie at his tailgate right there on the back side of the Holliday alumni parking lot partying like a rock star on game day just outside of Johnson Hagood Memorial Stadium. He has never been a guy to do anything for praise or public acknowledgment. He's just a genuine guy that loves The Citadel, the football program, and anybody that's a friend of the football family. He has taught me a lot about brotherhood and caring for your classmates. I hope all my classmates and former teammates know that I would drop anything for them in a heartbeat. That is what it means to be a Citadel man (or woman) and I along with The Citadel family appreciate everything Charlie has done for me, the football program, and most importantly for our great institution."

> *"It is amazing what you can accomplish
> if you do not care who gets the credit."*
>
> - HARRY S. TRUMAN

Chapter 17:

DOGS LOVE THE
TASTE OF CHICKEN

If you were born and raised in the state of South Carolina you grew up either hating the Gamecocks or loving them. I did not grow up in South Carolina, but I did not like those Gamecocks. I was indifferent toward them growing up; however, my disdain for them grew the moment I met some of their coaches, who wouldn't give me the time of day at recruitment time. Sure, I was only two hundred five pounds when I graduated from high school, but if you had seen my senior year highlights you would have thought that I played the game as a two-hundred-fifty-pound linebacker. Always remember, "It's not the size of the dog in the fight, but the size of the fight in the dog." One thing people underestimate when it comes to an underdog is the effect of the hunger burning inside of him and his untapped potential. I always believed that if I put my mind to it I could do it.

Speaking of underdogs, the next game on the schedule was with the SEC South Carolina Gamecocks at their home stadium in Columbia, SC.

We left for Columbia Friday morning and arrived at William Brice stadium early afternoon to walk around the field and warm up for about an hour. I remember Caleb, Kyle, Eric, Big Baby, and I getting together and taking pictures in front of the score board. We kept saying that finally the SEC would meet the SoCon. Big Baby couldn't help himself with his excitement and let out a roaring "LET'S GO!!" chant. Big Baby was known for two things on our team: for his famous "Let's Go" chants and being the only two-hundred-eighty-pound person in the state of South Carolina who could do a back flip off the ground in his full football uniform.

It was pretty cool being in the stadium visualizing myself making huge plays, sacking the quarterback while the crowd was cheering for the Bulldogs as we took down an SEC Goliath. For those that do not know about the history between USC and The Citadel, it goes back twenty-five years, to 1990. I remember hearing about it freshman year. According to Everett Sands, current running backs coach at USC, former running back for the 1990 Citadel Team, "One of the first things I remember was that morning of their game versus USC in 1990; in the (State) newspaper, it said all USC had to do to win was just show up, and the only way The Citadel could win was if Jack Douglas was Jamelle Holieway (of Oklahoma) and if The Citadel's wishbone was Oklahoma's wishbone. Coach Taaffe got us going off that. He was a great motivator." The Citadel beat USC 38-35. It was a heck of a game.

Two years later, in 1992, those same players were the ones who brought the team to the conference championship—the first time since 1961. The only thought in my mind during this time prancing around the field was that history had already repeated itself once this year with our winning a conference championship. It was destiny, fate, or whatever else you wanted to call it, but I just had this gut feeling that it was going to repeat itself again the next day. Everyone on the team wanted

to be remembered as the team that not only won a SoCon championship, but also as the team that beat South Carolina. It was a prophecy
in motion—a fate that had been written in the stars.

Media reporters who have never played the sport at the collegiate
level or higher should not be permitted to comment on matters such
as football. Sports commentators are simply observers in the stands,
while the athletes on the field are the ones doing all the work, sacrificing their time and energy, giving their blood, sweat, and tears to
pursue something much greater than themselves. My disdain for the
media grew after being disrespected by announcer Paul Finebaum the
previous year, who had said, "The Citadel vs Florida State is a cupcake
game. Florida State would have more competition playing a Texas high
school team." (Just to let the world know, we lost to FSU by only three
touchdowns. They were the number one team in the country, returning from a national championship with a Heisman Trophy-winning
quarterback, and we were a losing-record team that was FCS.) Luckily,
today we had a chance to change Paul's bias and get him to start respecting our program. For he was the sideline reporter for our game
that day and we couldn't wait to make him choke on his own words.
We were no cupcakes!

Respect, the most powerful word in the English language, is something earned, not given. It's funny how hubris has been the downfall
of many great titans and warlords throughout history. Achilles and his
heel, Goliath and a mere stone, Troy and the Trojan Horse, the list goes
on and on. Over time, the underdog wins because he wants it more
than his opponent does. His work ethic is stronger than his opponent's
skills and natural talents.

The next day, Saturday November 21, 2015 was game day! Before
leaving for the stadium, we had our morning routine of breakfast
and meetings at the hotel. Coach Drayton led the opening defensive

meetings. He was fired up. The opportunity had finally come. The Citadel Bulldogs had a chance to repeat history twenty-five years later.

Coach Houston barged in the door. "Fellas, look what's on the front page of today's *Columbia Times*."

"USC to focus on their game vs Clemson next week in order to be bowl eligible, not worried about playing The Citadel to save their season," the article read. It hit like a ton of bricks.

We, as a team, were tired of being compared to these Division I Power five schools and having games with us referred to as cupcake games or easy wins. We had had our chance to show Florida State University, the number one team in the country last season, that we were better than just a scheduled win, and we would do so again. We would make the *Columbia Times* eat their words. Now was our chance to stand up for our program and get some respect.

There was nothing but hubris that day in Columbia, South Carolina—the same lack of respect I had heard throughout my entire athletic career at The Citadel. The media just doesn't get it. They look only at tangibles, not realizing that a winner is much more than a forty time or how many times he can bench press. For example, look at Tom Brady. He ran the slowest forty-time at his NFL combine, and now he has won five Super Bowls. What do you think would happen if the Patriots had decided not to give him a shot because of his tangibles? There is no scientific method to discovering one's passion, emotion, and heart. The media had developed this mindset that our players were somehow inadequate because they were a little smaller, a little slower, this or that; well, keep giving us ammo and adding fuel to our fire. We knew what we're capable of, and we knew that day we were going to beat USC.

Our record was 7-3, 6-1 in the SoCon. In contrast, South Carolina had been struggling. They had recently lost longtime head coach Steve Spurrier.

Former two-time All-American UCLA football player Charles Arbuckle, Taylor Zarzour, and Paul Finebaum were the TV play-by-play analysts for the game.

I had done my homework to prepare for this game. Our entire team had. I had watched over eleven hours of film, studied scouting reports, and focused on my fundamentals such as stance, alignment, assignment, keys, and first step. The week's practices had been intense and grueling. Our will to prepare was greater than our will to win. That's the secret difference between champions and people that almost make it.

Coach blew the whistle. It was time to load up on the buses. We got on the bus and headed toward Williams Brice Stadium. On the way there I looked out the window. All I could see was burgundy, white, and black with the Gamecock symbol everywhere. There were tens of thousands of tents, RV's, cars, banners, coolers, and people tail-gating for this event. It wasn't yet 11:00 a.m. and I could tell some people were already drunk. I guess that's how they do it up here in Columbia, SC.

We arrived at the stadium, unloaded from the bus, and started getting ready for warmups. It felt like an eternity waiting in that locker room for pregame.

Only ten minutes left until kickoff. My legs were shaking, my palms were sweaty, my stomach was full of butterflies.

Coach called us up. I couldn't wait to hear his pregame speech. He could fire anyone up, even a watered-down plant. As we gathered up, the referee walked into the locker room. "Captains, we are ready." James, Kyle, Sam, and I went out to meet the referee before walking into the stadium for the coin toss. I remember my chest racing and adrenaline pumping. We walked into the tunnel, getting ready to walk out onto the field. The crowd was going crazy.

I was the call captain, which meant I was the first one to go out on the field to call heads or tails for the coin toss. The Gamecock captains were Pharaoh Cooper, wide receiver, who would later be drafted by the LA Rams as the hundred and seventeenth pick overall in the 2016 NFL Draft; Brandon Shell, offensive lineman, who would later be drafted by the New York Jets as the hundred fifty-eighth pick overall in the 2016 NFL Draft; Isaiah Johnson, free safety; and my old high school linebacker and brother TJ Holloman, inside linebacker, who would later be picked up by the Tennessee Titans.

We lined up in order: me, Sam, Kyle, and James. TJ, my old high school teammate, was USC's talking captain. As we walked to meet in the middle of the field, TJ and I looked each other in the eye. I gave him a head nod and a grin as we were walking to meet at the fifty-yard line. I couldn't help but think of all the good times we had shared playing with each other back at St. Pius X.

TJ and I were about to go head to head for the first time in our lives. He was on a team filled with four- and five-star recruits. On paper USC should blow us out of the water. At least, that was what my good friend Paul Finebaum thought. I remember the entire country talking about Pharaoh Cooper and how he was going to be an amazing NFL player. He was on the front page of the game day booklet, for Chrissake. Little did they know that we, The Citadel, had a bunch of hard-nosed smash-mouth football players that were hungry to prove to the world we belonged on this stage too. We might not have been four- or five-star recruits, but we played like it. It goes back to the old saying, "The hungrier dog will win," and let me tell you, we had an appetite for chicken.

We lined up on the fifty-yard line. Cameras from ESPN and the SEC network were in our faces during the toss. We won the toss and elected to defer to the second half. South Carolina chose to receive the ball. It was game time, baby!

All of the hard work I had put into playing this game since I was seven years old was about to pay off. We lined up to kick the ball off. Sandstorm was playing throughout the stadium; the crowd was jumping up and down. I could feel the stadium literally shaking to the music. Our goal was for the stadium to be silent come the fourth quarter of the game. Eric Goins started his motion to kick the ball. (Thud!) He kicked a high ball to the USC returner. He caught the ball and tried to gain some positive yards but was met by a pack of dogs at the twenty-one-yard line. (There was a flag on the play.) "Personal foul on number 81 on the Gamecocks." The referee moved the ball back to the eleven-yard line. As a defensive player, I could not ask for a better first and ten to play against on an opening drive. It was great field position for our team and terrible position for theirs.

The Gamecocks quarterback was Orth. His stats for the year included eight touchdowns, five interceptions, and he was 1-5 as a starter. Defensively, these were exciting numbers to hear. We needed to take advantage of his inexperience and pressure him to make errors on his own. Our team was known for being bloodhounds to the football. That season we had five defensive touchdowns and led the conference in forced fumbles and sacks. The first play of the game, Tevin called Eagle 4. He gave us a left call. I lined up in a seven technique between the tight end and tackle. Jerell Adams, USC tight end, who would later be drafted by the New York Giants, was lined up against me. He was a tall guy—about six foot six, weighing two hundred thirty-five pounds. I'm six foot two, two hundred forty-five pounds. I knew that I was stronger than him just by having a lower center of gravity and weighing more.

I just needed to use my technique and leverage my body to force him from blocking down on me. The ball was snapped. I could tell by the formation the Gamecocks were in that it was going to be a run play. Brandon Wilds, the running back, was lined up to my side in a "debby formation." "Debby" is a code term that means that the back is behind the quarterback. In this formation, I was expecting him to get the ball in an inside zone or isolation play. Either way our entire team knew he was getting the ball. "Down, set, hike!" Perry handed Wilds the ball. The tackle blocked down and Jerell Adams tried his best to block down on me and wash me out of the play. Unfortunately for him, I had done my homework and I was prepared for him to block down on me. I immediately stepped down with the tackle and drove my helmet underneath Adam's face mask. I used my hands to create separation from him and started driving my feet to close the gap behind him. Mitchell Jeter shot through the gap that was left from the pulling guard and dove at Wilds's feet to make the tackle.

I drove Adams into Wilds as he was being tackled. (Remember, it's all about the first punch.) I was just letting Adams know that I was going to be there all day and that he'd better bring it when he was going up against me. We could not let them get a first down on the first possession of the game. It was second and eight; Tevin called a right call. I lined up between Adams and Shell. This was a true testament to my ability to play the game against the best, because I was going against two future NFL draft picks. It couldn't get much better than that as far as competition goes. "Set, hike!" It was a run pass option play. Orth faked the handoff and threw the ball to Pharaoh Cooper. Q Washington, outside linebacker number 33, made a great play on Cooper and wrapped him up to make it third and one. The crowd was going crazy, all 77,500 fans jumping up and down. This was a defining moment in the game. We needed to dig deep and stop them to let them know it was going to be a full twelve-round boxing match. We needed to force them to punt. We had to make a big-time play on this down.

Coach Houston and Coach Drayton preached about stopping teams on third down. The keys for being a great defense are getting off the field as soon as possible and having your offense be the team that kills the clock. Remember I told you that third down is known as "money down" in our program. That's because in order to collect a paycheck after our work we have to stop the other team on money down. It was our chance to hit the Gamecocks square in their jaw and let them know that we are there to win! We were not a team they should have overlooked, even though they were going to pay us close to four hundred thousand dollars for playing that game. We were not going to simply just hand it over without a fight.

I was confident in our defense. Mitchell Jeter had 19.5 career sacks; Tevin, Mark, James, and Jonathan were ready to blow up any run in the middle. I figured our opponent, which was a much bigger team than us, was going to try to bully their way to a first down. The formation they were aligned in had the running back to my side in a debby formation. I was in a seven technique this time, between the tight end and Shell. I knew it was going to be an inside zone run play to me. All I needed to do was play my C-gap assignment and blow up the running back in the backfield. It was my time to shine!

"Ready, set, hike!" Orth handed the ball to Wilds. The tight end came crashing down on me, trying to wash me out. I simply gave him my right forearm to his face mask and put my shoulder underneath his chin. He fell to the ground. I was unblocked and in the backfield against Brandon Wilds. As he got the ball he saw me and tried cutting to the outside. "Not today!" I stopped him dead in his tracks and lunged forward as he was making his cut, grabbing him by his upper body and tackling him down for a two-yard loss.

We had just stopped the Gamecocks from getting a first down on the first drive of the game. With each play, we were getting more and more confident in that stadium. I jumped up from the tackle and looked over to our sideline at Coach Weaver and Russel Hubbs. I gave them a flex and did the hand motion in front of my face mask as if I were scooping up food and eating it. That is my signature move I go to after making a great play. I stole the move from Sean Witherspoon, a linebacker for the Atlanta Falcons. He and Keith Brooking were my football role models.

Complete shock. Everyone in the crowd could feel it. Our message to Columbia, South Carolina was "It's going to be a long day!" Shawn Kelly punted the ball to Schoultz. Schoultz caught the ball and got tackled immediately at the thirty-eight-yard line. Well, that is how you get a good first punch in there, but we needed to hit them with a combo and really let them know we were there to fight all the way until that clock hit 00:00. I ran off to the sidelines. It was time for the offense to do their thing.

It was our turn to take it to them. Assignment sound football is the only way a team can successfully defend the triple option. The moment a linebacker, defensive tackle, or defensive end does not play their assignment is the moment when all hell breaks loose and we make them pay for it.

I was anxiously watching with my teammates on the sideline. "Down, set, hike!" Dom hiked the ball and gave it to Cam Jackson for a three-yard gain. Our sideline was yelling and cheering them on. I was calling out to Sam Frye and Kyle Weaver to dominate the three-technique. It was second and seven; Dom hiked the ball and faked the handoff to Tyler as the defensive end crashed down. The outside linebacker scraped to attack Dom and forced the pitch to Cam Jackson. TJ Holloman scraped to tackle Cam Jackson; however, the USC safety did not do his job of setting the edge, and Cam had a clear lane to the end zone.

Bam! Vinny Miller made the prettiest cut on the outside linebacker and took him right out by attacking his knees. There was nobody around to stop Cam from getting to the edge and exploding down the sideline. Brandon Eakins, our wide receiver, made a clean block on the corner creating a lane between the numbers and the sideline. Cam was flying down the field the fastest I had ever seen him sprint. As he was running, I was running with him on the side line. He went the fifty, the forty, the thirty, the twenty, the ten. As he crossed the five-yard line, the backside corner, who had taken a great angle on Cam, lunged to tackle him. Cam leapt and dove from the four-yard line and brushed over the pilon before hitting out of bounds. The crowd was near hysteria. The referee looked to the other ref and gave the symbol....Touchdown! The Bulldogs had scored on the second play of the drive. "A fifty-nine-yard run." The crowd could not believe it. It was quiet except for that little section of blue going crazy in the corner of the stadium. The Gamecocks were shaken. By stopping them on their first drive, making them go three and out, and then turning around and scoring two plays later, we had had a great start. Oh boy, were they in for a treat. Rule number one: never underestimate your opponent!

Shawn Elliott, the interim coach, was probably saying "Oh, shit," to his coaching staff. Coach Houston was just silently smiling. We all were on the same page. The Dogs were there to play, and we played to win. There was a calm sense of confidence about our sideline.

Eric kicked the ball off. The Gamecocks put a six-play drive together and kicked a field goal, making the score 7-3 with 10:18 left in the first quarter. We got the ball back and put on a beautiful drive to answer. It was third and nine on the goal line. Dom hiked the ball. Mike Mabry blocked down on the defensive of tackle, creating a huge lane for Tyler to hit. Vinny made a great cut block on TJ, creating an even bigger lane to hit. Sam pulled behind Mabry and Vinny to punish the safety. All Tyler had to do was use his great speed and follow his blocks. Tyler hit the hole, breaking a tackle from the defensive end. The outside linebacker latched on to him, but it was too late. "Touchdown Citadel!" The Bulldogs' lead was 14-3 after Eric made the extra point.

The small Division I program from Charleston, South Carolina had just scored on its first two drives against an SEC school… talk about hard work and dedication. We had just put up a twelve-play seventy-yard drive to score on an SEC defense filled up with four- and five-star athletes. Our will was too strong. Everyone was shocked and couldn't believe what was happening. Everyone, even our fans. I looked over in the end zone and saw the look on Paul Finebaum's face. "The Citadel is running through South Carolina's defense," he finally announced. The surprise was palpable in his voice.

Eric kicked the ball off. The returner caught it and took off. The only thing about being successful early on in a game is that it can come back to bite you in the butt if you let your guard down. The kickoff team messed up on coverage; the returner was untouched and had an open lane to the goal line. All he had to do is get by Eric and then he'd be home free. The most disappointing thing ever is to lose a game because of special teams. An offense and defense can play lights out, but if our punt coverage or kickoff coverage messed up, it could cost us everything

It was between Eric and the four-star wide receiver. Luckily, our talented kicker Eric was a six-foot-two, two-hundred-ten-pound kicker, a former safety for the Oakton Cougars from Herndon, Virginia. He was no slouch at tackling. Our whole team was nervously watching as the returner, who had a sure shot at scoring, approached the thirty-five-yard line. All of a sudden, out of nowhere, Eric Goins made a touchdown-saving tackle—a textbook tackle, at that. Eric looked at the guy and shook his head. "Not today, buddy." The defense stopped the Gamecocks after an eleven-play drive resulting in a twenty-five-yard field goal. The score was 14-6 with twelve minutes left in the second quarter.

The rest of the second quarter was a back-and-forth battle. Each team was playing good defense. We held the Gamecocks to just another forty-one-yard field goal before going into the half. We ran back to the locker room and everyone was fired up. Coach Houston, Coach Drayton, Coach Weaver, and all of us were all on cloud nine; however, we as a mature team know that nothing mattered until that clock hit 00:00.

Everyone in the locker room was excited. Coach Weaver pulled the outside backers together, and we went over some plays that we had messed up defending in the first half. Dondray, Russ, Q, and I were having a great game. I slipped away to sit in my locker to visualize the second half. All I could think about was that clock hitting zero and the Bulldogs winning the game—the crowd of 77,500 people being dead silent while our blue-and-white fan section in the corner of Williams Brice Stadium chanted C-I-T-A-D-E-L, C-I-T-A-D-E-L, C-I-T-A-D-E-L. We had to win this ball game and show the world that The Citadel could beat an SEC team!

"The difference between a successful person and other is not a lack of strength, not a lack of knowledge, but rather a lack of will."

- VINCE LOMBARDI

Chapter 18:

IT'S NOT HOW YOU START, BUT HOW YOU FINISH

Before second half began, I glanced over at the sidelines of the Gamecocks. Coach Elliott was chewing their asses out. It must have been effective, because when we went back out to the field, our opponents seemed more determined and focused. Before the game had started, it was obvious that they did not respect us, but now that we had shown them who we really were, they were viewing our team as an in-conference opponent. I knew that they were going to come back swinging harder. Second half would be a dog fight.

The score stood at 14-9. The Gamecocks had more total yards and more first downs than we did. We had a hundred and ninety rushing yards and only three passing yards, yet we were scoring touchdowns while they were settling for field goals. Our defense's ability to bend but not break in the reds zone and our offense's ability to punish them on the ground and score touchdowns had kept our team alive.

USC kicked the ball off to us. It was a touchback. Time for us to get out on the battlefield and keep the upper hand. Dom hiked the ball and handed it off to Tyler Renew. He followed a great block by Kyle Weaver: It took four Gamecock defenders to bring him down after a twenty-yard rush. First and ten on our forty-yard line. Dom hiked the ball. Shit! Dom went the wrong way on the play. The backfield went right, and he went left. He was tackled for a four-yard loss by Jonathan Walton. Coach Houston was livid. We couldn't make mistakes like this if we were going to beat an SEC team. The next snap was a toss to Reggie Benjamin for an eight-yard gain. Now South Carolina, along with every other team in the country, knew that we rarely passed the ball. It was third down and four, and everyone on planet earth was thinking run. "Set, hike!" We handed the ball to Renew for a six-yard gain.

The great thing about our offense was that it gave our defense a lot of time to rest and killed the play clock. When you're ahead in a game, it's a great asset to have; however, when you are losing, it's tough to come back. We killed four minutes of clock and punted it back to South Carolina. Eric punted the ball to the five-yard line, but our gunners were not able to track it in time to stop it from rolling into the end zone. It was a great punt, but unfortunately, we could not communicate and down it inside the five-yard line.

First and ten, South Carolina on their twenty-five-yard line. They converted on a couple of pass plays and runs, making it first and ten from the forty-yard line. I looked at Brandon Shell. This guy was massive. He must've been six foot five, three hundred and fifteen pounds, and just straight muscle. His forearms were the size of my calves. He was a great blocker, and I was having a tough time getting a pass rush against him. Also, most of South Carolina's offensive plays were run-pass option plays, making it difficult to get a good pass rush. I had to play my run assignment before converting into the pass rush.

Assignment sound football and gap control is why we were so

successful on defense. "Set Hike!" Orth faked the hand off. Another run pass option. We played the run first, and then Orth launched the ball to Adams. Malik Diggs made a great play on the ball and almost intercepted it. (That would have been sweet, to get a pick in that stadium.) Third and seven. "Set, hike!" We were running a blitz from my side, coming fast, moving like freight trains about to attack Orth. He had to fire the ball out soon enough or get sacked for a major loss. We were bringing the pressure. James was about two steps away from making a huge sack when all of a sudden Orth released the ball and hit Pharaoh Cooper wide open on the seventeen-yard line going in. Dee ran him down and tackled him at the three-yard line. Crap! Those were the only plays that could hurt us. Dee never gave up big pass plays like that. It would happen no more than once or twice a season. He was the best corner in our league and projected as a top-ten defensive back in the entire Division I football.

We regrouped. It was first and three on our goal line. They were aligned in a heavy run formation. The blocking fullback had entered the game, and I knew that they were about to run the ball and try to punch it in. "Line down and compete" was our saying, and we couldn't break now. They ran to the other side of the field and gained two yards. Tackle made by Mitchell Jeter. Two and one. They ran the ball away from me again. I guess Russ and I were too physical for their TE, so to gain yards, they had to run away from us. "Set, hike!" They were running the same play, but to the opposite side. I stepped down because Shell stepped down. The tight end tried scooping me, but I pressured his inside shoulder, driving him back into the backfield. Orth handed the ball to Wilds. I had a clear shot to tackle him for a loss. I put my shoulder on his left quad and wrapped up. He wanted to get in the end zone badly. Not today. I tackled him for a zero-yard gain. I was fired up.

I made my signature eating gesture. Apparently, Charles Arbuckle and Taylor Zarzour liked my hand motion so much that they commented on how there is so much great food in Charleston. "Joe Crochet, haha, he says I want to eat. He says look you're not going to get in here. You got to come bring it. The South Carolina guys are saying ok we are down here. We are relaxed and Citadel is not giving them an inch. I love it! Junior from Stone Mountain, Georgia. Now there is great food in Charleston. You are absolutely right."

Third and one on the goal line with six minutes and thirty-five seconds left in the third quarter. We had to stop them there. We had to keep them out of the end zone. I was telling the D line to bring that stuff and keep fighting. It was a war in the trenches and we were the key to the puzzle if we were going to stop them from entering that end zone. They were lined up in the pistol formation. Orth was in shotgun and Wilds was behind him. Orth saw our defense and called an audible. He changed the play call. The play clock was going down five, four, three, two.... "Down, set, hike!" It was a G power to the opposite side of the field. We were outleveraged, and Wilds ran into the end zone. A loud cock-a-doodle-do sounded throughout the stadium, with an uproar of fans cheering and fireworks going off. South Carolina had just taken the lead for the first time in this game, making it 16-14.

We got the ball and drove it down the field to the thirty-eight-yard line. It was fourth and sixteen. Eric Goins set up for a forty-eight-yard field goal. This was longest field goal attempt of the season in one of the most crucial games of our career. If he made it, it would be the longest field goal made in his college career. I had faith in him. "Eric, you got this. You're the best kicker we got." We watched nervously from the sidelines. Dane, the holder, signaled to Hunter to snap the ball. Hunter snapped a great ball to Dane. Eric started his motion. (Thud!) He hit the ball square underneath the bottom quarter. It started its rotation.

As long as it got by the line of defenders and went untouched, the ball had a chance. The field goal team did a great job holding their water and preventing the Gamecocks from penetrating into the backfield to block the kick. The ball was rising, and from my angle it looked promising. As it went by the twenty-five, the fifteen, the five-yard line, I could feel the sweat pouring down my forehead. Time stood still as we watched that ball drift into the uprights. He made it! The two referees at the bottom signaled that it was good. Our entire sidelines went crazy and the little section of blue was almost as loud as the 77,500 Gamecock fans. We had regained the lead. 17-16 with ten minutes and twenty-six seconds left in the game. Coach Houston and Coach Weaver had the largest smiles on their faces.

"Eric Goins, junior from Herndon, Virginia. 3.9 GPA with an almost perfect field goal."

The strategy now was to stop them two more times and let our offense score one more time and then kill the clock. We kicked the ball of to them. They returned it to the twenty-six-yard line. "Set, hike!" Quick pass to the outside, a gain of four yards. "Set, hike!" Hand off down the middle to Shawn Carson, who broke through a missed tackle by Tevin and got tackled on the forty-nine-yard line. "Set, hike!" Missed pass. Second and ten. "Set, hike!" Orth completed a pass to Samuel for a first down. I looked at our guys; we were drained. We were playing an almost lights-out game, but physically we were tired this drive. Now would be a good time to call a timeout. "Set, hike!" We rushed Orth. It was a pass play. He let it fly down the middle of the field. Pharaoh Cooper on an inside post got past Diggy and caught the ball for a touchdown. A forty-one-yard completion. Dammit! Those were the only plays that could hurt us. They had not been able to drive the ball on us and score. Two big catches by Cooper had kept them alive. There were eight minutes forty seconds left in the game. The score was 22-17.

Instead of kicking a field goal, the Gamecocks were going for the two-point conversion. They were aligned in a shotgun formation with Trips and Wilde on the left—a formation we had not seen on film. We were thinking that the play call was going to be a run play to the field side or a short pick route pass play in the boundary where all the receivers were aligned. "Down!" Tevin started yelling at me, saying, "The ball is coming your way, Joe!" (Whistles started blowing.) Timeout, Gamecocks.

We huddled. Coach Tesh, Coach Taylor and Coach Weaver advised us to watch out for the bullshit—meaning trick plays. We needed to make sure to watch the ball because they might try to jump us offsides, and also a trick play could happen because they were not getting much yardage on the ground. Either way, we needed to be prepared for anything. We jogged out from the huddle. Everyone was mentally prepared for anything. We could not let them score, or the game could be out of reach. If we held them there, we could still win by making two field goals.

"Down!" They were in the same formation that they were in earlier; however, the trips and running back side was toward the field. "Set!" Orth motioned Adams from the tight end position to the field side. I was thinking heavy run on my side or pick route. However, something was fishy, because we had not seen this formation on film. Orth looked to the sideline for a long time. Something was up. "Hike!" He got the ball and started sprinting to his right toward the field side. The offensive line was just backpedaling. The defensive line was trying to get to Orth. All of a sudden, Orth just turned around and threw back to the left. There wasn't an eligible receiver on the left side!

"Who was he throwing it to?" Mary asked, and I was pleased (and a little bit surprised) that she could follow my football story.

All of a sudden, Big Brandon Shell caught the ball. Orth's pass went backward; therefore Shell could legally catch the ball and advance it. There was no one on that side to make that play. Oh, crap—he was about to score. Shell took a couple of steps toward the end zone. And then, out of nowhere, Shy Philips, a one-hundred-seventy-pound sophomore corner shot at Shell's ankles. He was our only chance to stop Shell from scoring. Shell tried to dodge Shy's hit, but Shy got him good, knocking him down at the nine-yard line! It was like watching a tree fall. He landed hard on the ground. Shy did it! He saved us. Had he not been there, Shell would have scored, resulting in a seven-point lead. I ran over to check on Shy. He was slow to get up. That boy he had knocked down weighed double what he weighed. It was great heads-up play. We still had a chance. I hustled to the sidelines to try and fire up the offense. I went up to Mike Mabry and Alex Glover. "Guys, I want to be on the team that was known for beating South Carolina." We all had that mentality. Just playing an SEC team competitively was mediocre. We were playing the game to win.

Eight minutes forty seconds left in the game. Gamecocks kicked the ball off. Another touchback. The crowd was louder than ever. "Game-Cocks, Game-Cocks, Game-Cocks!" Everyone was out of their seats. Dom rushed for a gain of four. Second and six. Tyler rushed for another first down. We had to score. It was going to take too long for our offense to make two field goals. Seven minutes, fifty-six seconds and the clock was ticking. "Down, Set!" Renew jumped. False start on the offense number 36. It was all right; We were still good. Next play Cam got the ball on a toss to the left side and made it second and four. Renew got the ball for a short gain. Third and short. The clock was still ticking.

A reason (other than sheer pride) for us to win this game was the implication it would have for the FCS playoff committee. Since we were co-conference champs, we were not guaranteed to be in the FCS playoffs. We were still on the fence with the committee.

"Down!" Dom saw a gap in the Gamecocks' formation. He audibled and changed the play. "Set, hike!" He handed the ball to Tyler Renew. Kyle Weaver and Isaiah Pinson drove the defensive tackle five yards off of the line of scrimmage. Coach Boyd was going to love this play on film. Tyler followed his block. Reggie scooped the defensive end, creating a lane between Isaiah and Reggie. The only Gamecock players that could stop Tyler were TJ and the other inside linebacker. TJ set the edge. It was just Tyler and the other linebacker. The player overran the play. Tyler broke free on the forty-eight-yard line with a straight shot to the end zone. There was no way anyone was stopping this kid from scoring. He went the forty, the thirty, the twenty, the ten. Touchdown, Bulldogs! We did it. We had regained the lead!

I looked over at my family and Emily in the jumping, screaming crowd. Emily was wearing the lucky jersey. Fate was on our side. It was almost prophetic the way this season had turned out. We were up 23-22. We had to go for two in order to make it a three-point score difference. There were still six minutes and seven seconds remaining. We ran a full-back toss to the right side, and Tyler was stopped at the line of scrimmage.

Offense did their job; now it was up to the defense to do ours. Coach Houston pulled us outside, rage visible in his face. "All right, guys—play assignment football, do your jobs, and play hard. Big stop here." We kicked the ball off. The butterflies were back. We had six minutes and seven seconds to determine if we would go down in history as one of the greatest teams in Citadel football. I kept thinking about Tim Tebow's speech: "Thirty minutes for the rest of our lives, thirty minutes for the rest of our lives." It truly is a testament to your hard work and dedication to come down to the wire in an SEC stadium, beating a team that overlooked all of our players when they were recruiting in high school.

"Set, hike!" Orth completed a pass to Cooper for twenty-one yards. The clock was still ticking. The next play they gained seven on a pass play to Cooper. We had to stop Cooper. "Set, hike!" the Gamecocks were in hurry-up offense. They were trying to tire us out so we would make a mistake that would give a big play. Quick passes and no huddle offense is a deadly recipe. However, we were tougher and more conditioned. No gain on the quick pass play. Third and three, four minutes, forty-eight seconds remaining. They handed the ball off and get two yards. It was fourth down and one on our own forty-seven-yard line. This was where great teams shine. We had to stop them there. Another first down would put them in field goal range. "Set, hike!" They ran an inside zone to the read side. All they had to get was a yard, and then they would be in field goal position to win the game. The running back got the ball. He had a clean hole to get the first down.

Suddenly, out of nowhere, Mark Thomas made a phenomenal play in the backfield. (Bam!) Mark hit the running back two yards in the backfield. He started driving his feet, but so did the running back. Each split second, more and more dogs were banging their helmets on the running back, forcing him to the ground. We made the stop. Bulldogs' ball!

"Now you're telling me an SEC running back cannot get a yard," one of the announcers commented. That's how the dark-side defense plays. Eleven guys running to the ball with a bad attitude. That is textbook defense right there. There were four minutes and seven seconds left in the game. All our offense needed to do was hold on to the ball and kill time off the clock. Against Davidson, we were able to kill six minutes of the game clock easily. We could definitely do it here, especially with the way our team had been playing all game. I looked into the crowd on the sidelines. Every single Gamecock fan was shaken. The crowd was starting to quiet down. Hope, the single most essential quality that allows any human being to thrive during a dark time, was fading quickly for them. Cam got the ball for a seven-yard gain. Yes! We ran the same play again and Cam got a gain of two. Third and one yard to go. We had to convert this and another first and ten in order to seal the game. South Carolina had two timeouts left.

"Set, hike!" Dom handed the ball to Renew on a full-back dive. (Bam!) The defensive tackle burst through the line and stopped Tyler a little after the line of scrimmage. The referee's call for a measuring timeout. The sticks came out. Every player on the sidelines was crossing their fingers and praying to God that we got the first down. "Lord, please let us get this first down. We have played our butts off and deserve to win this game."

The measurement came down to the inches. Luckily, we got the first down by a hair. First and ten for the Dogs. Two minutes and thirty-seven seconds left in the game. The clock was ticking. With fifteen seconds left on the play clock, Dom hiked the ball. "What are you doing?" yelled Coach Houston. Dom, I guess, was nervous and forgot that killing time is the name of the game. He got hit in the backfield for a two-yard loss. Timeout South Carolina. Two minutes twenty-five seconds left in the game. Our team went to the side line to regroup and receive a pep talk from Vinny Miller.

"Set, hike!" Tyler got a three-yard gain up the middle. Timeout South Carolina. That was their last timeout of the game. It all came down to this play to seal the game. If not, the defense would have to make another stop. Coach Weaver called me over. "All right, Joe, I need you guys here. We are going to have to go out there one more time. It comes down to us." In that moment I thought back to the days when I in fifth grade on the Tucker Lions team. We beat the Sandtown Vikings for the hundred-and-twenty-pound Pop Warner championship. I remember at the beginning of the season Coach Anthony Maddox calling my dad constantly asking if I could come play for the team. In my mind, I was a baseball player. I had signed up for fall baseball and did not think of playing football ever again. Until I went to the jamboree day and watched the team that I had played for struggling against the other team. That's when I realized that I missed football so much. Coach Anthony came up to me and said, "We could have used you out there and really want you to come back." Who was I fooling? I was not a baseball player; I was a football player. I showed up to practice the next week and I remember Coach Anthony saying, "Joe, you are going to lead my team to a championship."

I don't know why I reverted back to that memory at that moment—such a crucial time in the game. Maybe it was a sense of having others depending on me. Either way, it fired me up and I remember calling the defense together and saying, "This is the last drive of the game. We stop them here, we win. Simple as that. What is your why? This is the time of the game when you play for your why the most. We owed it to our whys and for everyone who has supported us to be here in this moment, to give it everything we have and then some for this last two minutes of the game." I looked into James Riley's eyes. He was on another planet. He looked like a pissed-off Ray Lewis ready to knock the head off the running back or receiver that went his way. Mitchell Jeter's fists were clenched; he was more focused than ever. Mark, Tevin, Coop, Jon Jon—everybody knew what we had to do. Our whole defense was ready to prove to the world that the SoCon took down an SEC school at their home field.

Defense wins championships and big-time games. Third and nine for the Dogs. The crowd was back on their feet. That one drop of hope formed into a puddle and all 77,500 people were jumping up and down, yelling at the top of their lungs, waving towels in the air. It was super loud on that field.

"With one more first down, the Bulldogs will put the game on ice," said Zarzour.

"The replay function has malfunctioned… there will be no replay."

Everyone was waiting for what felt like hours. The time continued to tick away as we were waiting for the referees to get the game going again. Five more minutes went by. It felt like an eternity. The replay function needed to be worked out. After a couple of minutes (whistle blew), "Game's back on." We had thrown the ball three times total this entire game. If you haven't figured it out yet, our bread and butter was running the football. (I think by now even my little cousin who is in elementary school knows that we were just going to keep running the ball.) "Down, set, hike!" Dom kept the ball following Tyler on a quarterback power. He gained two yards on the play; however, we needed six to get a first down. It was fourth and four on our forty-four-yard line. One minute thirty-five left in the game. My palms were sweaty and my heart was racing. "Timeout," yelled coach Houston.

I ran over to the defense. "Guys, it's up to us." I looked directly into Mitchell and Mark's eyes. We were ready. "Defense wins championships, and it all comes down to us to prove to the world that history can and will repeat itself." Will Vanvick got back to punt. (Bam!) He punted a perfect ball between the left hash and numbers. Aaron Spann caught the ball at South Carolina's three-yard line. We could not have asked for a better field position.

"Good job, Will!" I said as I ran onto the field. I took a deep breath, taking in the moment. All week I had visualized this moment: being on the field and stopping USC to win the game. I had a feeling that I was going to make a huge play—maybe an interception if Coach let me drop back into coverage. The Gamecocks had zero timeouts left and had to drive the ball more than fifty yards to get into field goal range. On top of that, they still had to make a field goal or score with one minute twenty-six seconds left in the game. Fate was on our side; however, I have never believed in luck other than its true definition, which is preparation meeting an opportunity. Defensively, we were mentally prepared for the hurry-up offense and quick passes. The only way they could beat us was with a deep ball to Adams or Cooper downfield.

It was first and ten on the three-yard line. They lined up in a double-wide formation with a back in the backfield. I knew they were trying to get a quick pass in this play. They could either quick pass and march down the field or go for the big shots.

"Set, hike!" We blitzed on the right side. I dropped back into zone coverage. My responsibility was the hook curl. As I was dropping back into my zone, I began thinking, *I am going to get a pick here to end the game.* I was dropping off of the number 2 receiver. He ran a ten-yard straight then out route to the sideline. I jammed him at seven yards while keeping my eye contact on Orth. I saw Adams, who lined up as the number one receiver, cut behind the guy I was dropping off of and broke in front of him, knowing that he was Orth's go-to target. As I was breaking to Adams, Orth got smashed by Mitchell Jeter while he was releasing the ball. I was in perfect position to pick the ball off. Dee was right behind me, breaking on the duck of a ball Orth threw. Either Dee or I was going to get pick this ball off.

I dived and reached my hand out for the ball but fell inches shy of catching it. Dee was in the same boat. Our defensive pressure kept Orth from stepping into the throw and forced him to throw a crappy low ball. If Mitchell wasn't as good at his job, I might have been able to pick the ball off. It is funny, I have not gotten an interception since middle school in a game. I have been cursed. The last interception I had was in sixth grade when I was playing for the Tucker Lions.

I dived, trying to make a one-handed grab, and missed the interception by inches. Dammit, that was my chance. We could have ended the game right there. Dee was within inches from it behind me as well. I got up from the ground and all of a sudden, I started feeling this sharp pain in my back. Not only had I missed the interception, but I had landed poorly on my lower back.

Crap, there was only one minute and twenty-two seconds left in the game. I couldn't go out now. Not in a game like this. I took a step and the pain crawled up my spine. Coach Weaves saw me holding my back and sent in Russ for the next play. "Coach, I have to be out there… this is what I have been working toward my entire career."

Coach Weaver looked at me. "Joe, catch your breath; we are going to need you if they get a first down, and I want you to be as fresh as possible in case they do."

Thank God I had a great back-up. Russ had been playing lights out this entire game. He had had two tackles for loss and had not missed an assignment yet.

"Coach, I'm fine… let me back into the game! I need to be on that field and help my brothers close this out." It was second and ten, another pass play. We dropped everyone back into coverage, leaving only a three-man rush. Orth had way too much time to find his open receiver. Mark and Mitchell were the best defensive rushers in the SoCon, and even they were having a hard time against this SEC line to make penetration. Orth passed to Pharaoh Cooper on the right-side line. Mariel Cooper, CB for our team, made a great play on the ball and smacked it out of Pharaoh's hands. It was third down and ten—only two more stops, and we would win! Russ stayed in because it would take too long to sub in.

I was yelling on the sidelines. I could barely watch. I knew I needed to be out there. Orth hiked the ball and passed it to Deebo Samuel. Dondray Copeland dropped back into the curl covering the curl-flat. Dray broke on the ball and beelined it toward Sanders. Sanders reached to catch it. "Not today," said Dondray. He grabbed Sanders and tackled him for a three-yard gain. It was fourth and seven from the six-yard line. Sanders stayed inbounds, so the clock was still running.

The Gamecocks had zero timeouts left. We were playing lights-out defense. "Coach, put me in. I'm good!"

Without hesitation, I ran onto the field and subbed Russ out. I had worked my whole entire life for this moment, and I wasn't going to let a little pain in my back prevent me from being out there and helping my team be victorious. It's a defensive player's dream to be out there in a game time situation like this. "Fourth and seven. Game on the line," said Zarzour. USC snapped the ball; we were blitzing everyone. Coach Drayton called for our defense to rush six and try to pressure Orth to make a bad throw.

Orth made a quick pass out of the backfield. (Wild whistling from the referees.) I stopped playing, because the referees stopped the game; however, our secondary could not hear the whistle being blown with all of the noise from the crowd. Cooper caught the ball from Orth and took off. Nick Willis continued to play the game also, for he didn't know the game was dead either.

What was going on? Everyone had stopped playing, except for Nick and Pharaoh. Our whole sideline was silent. Nick ended up diving at Pharaoh's legs and missed the tackle, allowing Cooper to walk into the end zone.

"Wow, did they really just score?" Mary asked. She was really wrapped up in the story.

"Hang on," I said. "Let me finish."

The crowd was going crazy. We were on the field looking around, not knowing what to think. The referee had blown his whistle multiple times. The play had been ruled dead; however, nobody else in the stadium could hear the whistle, and everyone thought that we had just lost the game. There was no way they had just scored. I thought, *Did we just lose the game?*

No one knew what was going on. There were forty seconds left in the game. We were disheveled and did not know what to think. All of a sudden, I looked to my right and there was a penalty flag between the number and the sideline at the line of scrimmage. They must've false started; the penalty had to be on them. We couldn't just lose a game like that. I looked over at the Gamecocks, and they were pissed. Orth had a devastated look on his face. The referees huddled together. The game field judge broke away from the huddle to face the crowd. "Not all of the eleven players on the offense were set; therefore, that turns into a false start. That's a five-yard penalty, replay fourth down." With the clock running and inside of one minute, there would be a ten-second runoff. The clock was reset to forty-two seconds. The crowd was going berserk, booing left and right. Nobody could believe what had just happened. Everybody on the field heard the whistle, but it was just crazy how one eight-second play could have had such a detrimental effect. Luckily, we were the more disciplined team.

It was fourth and ten. The clock continued to run. The Gamecocks were in a double-wide formation with one running back in the back field. Orth snapped the ball. Defensively we called a cover eight zone. My responsibility was to drop back in the curl. At this point, we could not let them complete a deep ball or get the first down. James and I saw Wilds sneak out of the backfield. Orth threw the ball to Wilds. We both broke toward the ball, like piranhas attacking a bloody fish in the middle of the Amazon River. He caught the ball at the six-yard line and took off. James closed from the left side and tackled him at the ten-yard line. I was right there, inches away in case he broke his tackle.

Immediately James and I both looked to the chains to see if USC got the first down. Wilds was short by a yard of the first down. We had done it! We'd beat the South Carolina Gamecocks 23-22! I looked over to the sidelines and everyone was going crazy. Our Citadel section was chanting C-I-T-A-D-E-L, C-I-T-A-D-E-L, C-I-T-A-D-E-L. We had just shocked the world for the second time this season. History had just repeated itself twenty-five years later. The SoCon beat the SEC Goliath. The announcer exclaimed, "Mike Houston in his second season as the head coach of The Citadel Bulldogs delivers the biggest win in a quarter of a century in Charleston."

We took off to our sideline to cheer. We raced onto the field in amazement. It was unreal, like a dream. We ended up getting a penalty for unsportsmanlike conduct by having too many people on the game field, but nobody cared.

We lined up, and Dom took a knee. It was icing on the cake or the last nail in USC's coffin. We stormed the field in celebration. Our players took off to find coach Houston to dump Gatorade on him.

Paul Finebaum ran over to coach, "Coach, twenty-five years ago The Citadel beat South Carolina. You did it again today?" Coach Houston looked at Paul.

"Well, twenty-five years ago didn't help us today, but I've got a tough bunch of kids that believe in each other, believe in doing things right on and off the field, and they played their guts out today."

"Coach, no one gave you a chance; how did you get it done?"

Coach Houston looked directly into Paul's eyes. "I told you, they're a tough bunch. They come to practice every day, they did a great job executing our game plan there. I mean the headline of the Columbia paper today said that we had no chance. Twenty-five years ago, they said the same thing. At some point they better start respecting the kind of young men that we have at The Citadel."

"What will this mean for your program?" Finebaum asked.

"It means we're going to the playoffs. So, we better get ready to play next week."

Tyler was named the player of the game with twenty-three rushes, a hundred and seventy-four yards, and two touchdowns. It was a dream of a lifetime. He was from Columbia, South Carolina and as a kid he used to sell peanuts in this very stadium. He had a lot of soul and passion for playing in his hometown. The devil himself didn't stand a chance of stopping this boy today. It was a dream come true for all of us, but most importantly for him. I know his mom, who passed away many years ago, was out there beside him on that field that day.

In the locker room all the players were hugging each other. "Knuck if you Buck" started playing and we started jumping up and down, going crazy. More music came on in the background. By this time all of the cameras and cell phones were out, documenting the moment. We started singing the lyrics and turning up. We all knew that we would soon be partying like rock stars and celebrating in downtown Charleston.

Coach Houston walked in and yelled, "How 'bout them Bulldogs?" We all started cheering. I still couldn't believe that we had done it. He continued, "I'm telling you, you guys are the most amazing group of young men I have ever coached in my entire life. You believed in each other, you believed in the coaching staff, and you worked your butts off, and you earned a victory over a SEC opponent at their place. At some point they are going to quit disrespecting us in the Columbia paper. This is evidence that when you do the right thing on the field and off the field, you work together, you play together, you love each other, you can beat anybody." I could not agree more.

We had only six hours to celebrate this win, and then it would be time to focus on the playoffs!

"The ones who want to achieve and win championships motivate themselves."

- MIKE DITKA

Chapter 19:

FALL MADNESS:
THE FCS PLAYOFFS

O ur win over South Carolina, along with our tying for first place in the Southern Conference, gave the FCS Playoff Committee more than enough reason to put us in the dance. The last time The Citadel had gone to the FCS playoffs was in 1992, and the team had never won a road playoff game. But because we lost to Chattanooga, it was guaranteed that we would be playing away. Either way, we were excited to be making history and ready to prove to the world that The Citadel was going to win the national championship.

The FCS Playoff selection was being broadcasted on ESPN U nationally and we watched it together in the Altman Center at the South end of Johnson Hagood Memorial Stadium. The top eight teams in the country are exempt from the first playoff game, while teams ranked number nine through sixteen teams have home field advantage, and teams ranked seventeen through twenty-four are relegated to playing away. With The Citadel ranking in at number eighteen, we knew we would have to travel.

The selection show was a blast, both the watching and the filming. (They had sent a crew to livestream us when The Citadel's ranking was announced.) There were cameras, microphones, food, beverages, and a huge screen showing the event on ESPN U. All the coaches, their families, parents, and committed alumni were at this event. Coach inspected our physical appearance and clothing to make sure we were up to Citadel standards in our team's blue-collared shirt, sweat pants, and team shoes. It was all pretty hectic, and definitely exciting. We had just beat South Carolina the day before, thrusting us into playoffs, and now here we were being filmed and watching the selection show, and at 2:00 p.m. we'd be right back to our usual Sunday postgame routine: the usual weight lifting, meeting, and practice schedule, which wouldn't end until around 8:30 p.m. At this level you have to love the game, because it requires a lot of sacrifice!

After grabbing some food and drinks, we sat down to watch the selection show. "Welcome to the NCAA FCS Football Championship Selection Show." They started off showing schools such as James Madison, North Dakota State, Jacksonville State, and McNeese State. The team favorite to win it all that year was North Dakota State. Their record was 9-2 and they had consecutively won the last four NCAA FCS National Championships. "The brackets are out. Number one, Jacksonville State; Number two, Illinois State; Number three, North Dakota State; Number four, McNeese State; Number five, James Madison; Number six, Portland State; Number seven, Richmond, and number eight, Charleston Southern."

It was a slap in the face that Charleston Southern had made it to the top eight in the country. We led during our entire game and should have beaten them. That should be us up there, and they should be having to travel instead of hosting a second-round playoff game. The ESPN U production guy yelled, "Everyone we're about to air. When

I give you the ready, start cheering and clapping facing the screen. We're about to go live in three, two, one...." We all started clapping our hands and cheering. On the screen the host of the show said, "All right, let's continue to unveil the brackets. Chattanooga is set to play Fordham at 1:00 p.m. in Chattanooga, and Coastal Carolina will host The Citadel Saturday at 2:00 p.m." We started going crazy. During preseason, Coastal had been projected as the number one team in the country, but they had lost to Charleston Southern. We had played Coastal the year before as our home opener and got embarrassed. It was time for some payback.

Fortunately, Coastal ran a very similar offense to that of South Carolina and every shotgun run-pass option team we had faced that past season. The depth of the back, stance of the offensive lineman, number of tight ends, and play recognition from tape made it easier as a defense to predict the plays; however, they had three options every time they snapped the ball. They could pass it, hand it off, or the quarterback could keep it for himself.

A lot of running is involved for a defense to react and make plays, especially if the team has a hurry-up tempo offense and doesn't give us a chance to rest between plays. Either way, our pathway to a national championship had been set. We had to beat Coastal Carolina in Conway, South Carolina, then beat Charleston Southern, play Chattanooga or Jacksonville State, and then play two more games after that to become the number one team in the country.

Our team had a great week of practice. After knocking out our responsibilities in the Corps and in the classroom, we were set for making history. We got on the bus Friday to travel two hours and twenty-five minutes northeast to North Myrtle Beach. I'd been there a couple times and found it quite pleasant—much more to my liking than the adjacent and overly commercialized Myrtle Beach; and, it just so happened that Emily's family owned a town house in North Myrtle Beach, so that was certainly convenient.

Our bus pulled up to Beach Cove Resort, which would be our home for the next two days. Man, were we in for a treat! I never dreamed I'd be staying at a vacation resort for an away game. Talk about a distraction! Each of our rooms had an ocean view, a huge living room, a balcony, a kitchen, and a bedroom. The property featured an outdoor pool with a lazy river, an indoor pool, a hot tub, and access to the beach. What more could a guy ask for? (I know what you're thinking, and I already have an answer to that, because my girl and her family were staying ten minutes away at their place.)

November 28th, 2015: We woke up and went through our morning routine of film, walkthroughs, devotional, and pregame meals. From there we made the thirty-minute drive to Conway. This was my first time ever visiting or seeing Coastal Carolina University, which I had heard was a party school with beautiful girls.

We played Coastal Carolina very hard. It was an offensive matchup. Neither team could stop the other from scoring. The Chanticleers had scouted our play calls and knew what plays we were running defensively. Coach Drayton signaled a cover eight zone play in which I was supposed to drop back into coverage. I knew the play call and I knew my assignment, but for some reason I rushed the quarterback, Alex Ross, who was surprised by my move. He made a bad throw where Shy Phillips picked off the pass and returned it for a thirty-two-yard touchdown. When I got to the sideline Coach Drayton came up to me and said, "Joe, it's all God's plan. I didn't call that play, but it worked out in our favor. Keep working."

We continued to battle it out. As the clock was winding down with less than a minute to go in the fourth quarter, the score was 38-38. Coastal had the ball for what seemed like the final drive of the night. We could not stop them. They were passing all over us. "Down, set, hike!" Ross snapped the ball and Tevin Floyd rushed the quarterback and strip-sacked Alex Ross, which Mitchell Jeter recovered. This set us up for the possible winning score. It all came down to Eric's forty-three-yard field goal at the end of the game to seal the victory. Hunter snapped the ball to Dane, who was holding for Eric. Eric started his motion. Coastal's defense was penetrating our offensive line. (Wham!) Eric kicked the ball and it started to rise. A Coastal defensive player jumped to block the kick, but thankfully missed the ball by inches. The ball continued to soar through the uprights as time expired. We had won the game 41-38! Everyone stormed the field and tackled Eric, making what we referred to as a "huge dog pile" on the fifty-yard line. Another record in the record books for this 2015 season with the first road playoff win in school history! We were now 9-3 and our next game was against none other than Charleston Southern University.

We played CSU very well. Unfortunately, though, we did not win. I had my best game ever in my career that day, as did most of our defense, but we still ended up losing 14-6. We stopped them the entire game. Only two plays, where the running back broke free and scored, lost us the game. If we could have taken out those two plays we would have won. The hardest part about this loss was that we had given it everything we had and still fell short.

"Wait, is that the end of your season?" Mary asked.

I looked out my window. The plane had lowered in altitude. I could see the earth unfurling beneath the window. "It was the last game I ever played with Mitchell, Mark, James, Nick, Coop, Sam, Mike, Vinny, Brandon, Alex, Caleb, Eric, Hunter, and Dane."

It was the end of the class of 2016 era. Little did I know that the tides in Charleston, SC were about to change again—for better or worse was yet to be determined.

"Ladies and gentlemen, we are about to begin our initial descent into Atlanta. If you could please return your seats and tray tables to their original upright positions now," a flight attendant announced.

"I've been a very lucky guy. I played on championship teams... I've won some awards and I'm very proud of those accomplishments. But I don't think there's anything greater than to come home and to be recognized at home. This is the pinnacle."

- BOBBY ORR

Chapter 20:

MY WINNING
SEASON BANQUET

A celebratory banquet was held for us during spring semester. Attending this banquet, for me—for all of us, probably—was bittersweet. Sweet because we were champs and we deserved the recognition; but also, a bit sad because Coach Houston and Coach Weaver had both left The Citadel to coach at James Madison University. I know now that it is common for coaches to change teams after a couple years. Better opportunities come along for the coaches, or they may be fired. Whatever the reason, it's not unusual for some of the team members to feel a sense of resentment when their coach moves on. Several of the players on my team, for example, expressed that they felt they had been used for the coaches' résumé material. I mean who wouldn't want to hire a coach that had led The Citadel team to victory?

You can't blame anyone for wanting to improve their lifestyle, but I think Coach Houston's departure could have been handled differently. Fortunately, I was able to talk with him before he left. He said goodbye and apologized for the abrupt news; however, there were ninety other players he did not talk with individually.

Let this be a lesson for those planning on playing college football: It's important to make your decision about which school to play for based on what you value in an institution. Don't base your decision on how much you like the coach, because you never know how long he'll be there.

The banquet was attended by over four hundred and fifty people. The highlights of the event included the presentation of our Southern Conference championship rings and recognition of seventy-five lettermen, with an additional recognition given to the twenty-two seniors who had played their final season.

Head coach Brent Thompson (former offensive coordinator who had taken over as new head coach) closed the ceremony with remarks reflecting on the team's success before instructing each cadet-athlete to open their box and unveil the Southern Conference Championship ring.

The program also included recognition of seventy-five lettermen, in addition to honoring each of the twenty-two seniors who played their final season at The Citadel in 2015.

I was honored to receive the CoSIDA Academic All-American plaque after becoming the first Bulldog since 1989 to earn first-team Academic All-American honors.

Other individual and group honors were awarded. The Citadel starting offensive line, consisting of left tackle Isaiah Pinson, left guard Kyle Weaver, center Ryan Bednar, right guard Frye and right tackle Michael Mabry, earned Offensive Player of the Year honors.

Linebacker Tevin Floyd was named Defensive Player of the Year. Kicker Eric Goins earned Special Teams Player of the Year honors. James Riley took home the CFA Blood & Guts award.

B-Back Tyler Renew was given the Brigadier Foundation Award for Team Before Self.

Defensive lineman Jonathan King won the Linwood Sikes Award for outstanding effort. Defensive lineman Mark Thomas was given the Cal McCombs Award.

A-Back Cam Jackson earned the Ann Seignious Award for Academic and Football Excellence.

Quarterback Dane Anderson was recognized for his service as team military captain.

Quarterback AJ Vandiver was named Offense Scout Team Player of the Year.

Defensive back J.J. Baldwin was the team's Defense Scout Team Player of the Year

Linebacker Za'Von Whitaker took home Special Teams Scout Team Player of the Year.

The Bulldogs finished the season with a 9-4 overall record and were named co-champions of the Southern Conference with a 6-1 mark in conference play. They were ranked thirteenth in the nation in the final STATS poll and fifteenth in the final coaches' poll. The Citadel won its first conference championship since 1992 and advanced to the NCAA FCS playoffs for the first time since that same season. The Bulldogs' six conference wins tied the program record, and the nine wins overall was the second-highest single-season total in program history.

EPILOGUE

Though many players received well-deserved recognition for their individual performances, it was a team effort that enabled this magical season to unfold. It took every one of our hundred and thirteen players, the seventeen coaching staff personnel, the support of the alumni, The Citadel Corps of Cadets, and the friends and family of our players to accomplish this amazing feat. None of this could have happened, however, without God. I give him all the credit and all the glory.

Despite having graduated twenty-two seniors, the class of 2016 was able to lead The Citadel to its first conference championship since 1992. Not only were we a group of outstanding football players, but we were better men. This class was the first group of men to truly buy into the process and make the sacrifices necessary to become champions. Remember the iceberg analogy—a lot more goes into play than what everyone sees. This class has set a precedent for many classes to follow. This class, along with every man on this roster, will be remembered as champions. A lot of people believe that The Citadel class ring is the most valuable ring at this great institution. I beg to differ because only one hundred thirteen people in the entire world will ever have a 2015 SoCon Championship Citadel ring.

I'm going to miss this great group of guys. Even though there is one more season left in my story, I will never again be in the same room again with most of these guys. Even though time is going to create distance between us, it will not diminish what we share. We share a bond that cannot be broken or forgotten. It puts things in perspective the day you hang up the cleats. Fortunately, I had one more season: my red-shirt senior year. Along with the other seniors such as Kyle, Dray, Cam, Tevin, Schoultz, Ryan, and Will, I must take responsibility for continuing what my class, the class of 2016, started and ensuring that The Citadel will win another Southern Conference championship.

The plane had reached terra firma and was taxiing to the gate.

"You sure did have a great experience at The Citadel," Mary said, smiling.

Her mom looked over at me. "Thank you for entertaining her on this plane ride. It was great listening to an actual first-person perspective of being a college football player, a cadet, and a student. I think you really have inspired Mary to chase her dreams. My husband talks about The Citadel all the time, but I never really heard an athlete's perspective."

"Yes ma'am, and you are welcome. It was not a problem for me at all to reflect on those memories. Thank you for letting me share my experience. I enjoyed passing the time with you both. I hope she can get some valuable information from this and use it as motivation to make a difference. I look at her and say it is an amazing realization to know that one person can change the world and it is even a more divine experience to realize that that person is the person you look at every day in the mirror."

I turned to Mary. "One day you'll go to college and see the importance of getting a great education. You'll meet friends that you will cherish for life. Heck, who knows… maybe one day you'll go to The

Citadel and be able to make a tremendous impact on at that institution like my classmates and I did."

She looked at me with a huge smile on her face. "I want to go to college. I love Penn State, but I also really like Clemson. Either way, I want to join a school and be a bioengineer. After that, I want to be in the medical field helping others."

"Well, I'm sure you'll do great!"

The plane came to a stop. The fasten seat belt sign turned off and the aisle filled with passengers hurrying to grab their bags from the overhead compartment and make their way off the plane into the super-busy Atlanta airport. (The busiest in the world, in fact.)

As I was standing in the aisle, waiting for those in front of me to move, I thought about how great it was meeting this young girl and her mother. I love meeting new people. My goal in life is to positively impact everyone I meet. If I can do that, then I'm following God's plan. No matter what happens or when it happens, when I'm fortunate to meet another human being, it is a blessing. God had crossed our paths and there was a reason for that. I truly believe in God's purpose and hope that I accomplished His will by speaking to this young girl and her mom through my story.

To my readers, I hope you understand that the ultimate value of life is bringing love, joy, and happiness to others. Money and material goods are not the sole purpose of why we are on this planet. I'm not saying you shouldn't try to be financially successful, but if all you care about is attaining wealth, then what truly is your purpose?

I debarked the plane and headed toward baggage claim, feeling excited about seeing my family and my dog Tucker.

Getting out of the Atlanta Airport can be a real pain in the butt. I had to ride a train from Terminal C to the stop for baggage claim. From there I followed the hordes of people up an extremely long escalator. As

I ascended, I heard a familiar voice, "Hey Mister Joe… Mister Joe?" It was Mary, calling from behind. "You forgot something." She held up my phone. In the excitement of our goodbyes, I'd forgotten to grab it from the pouch on the back of the seat in front of me.

"Oh my gosh, thank you! I'll get it from you at the top of the escalator." We get to the top of the escalator and she handed me my phone. "Thank you for grabbing that. I know three people that would be very mad at me if I didn't have it." Mary and I high-fived.

"Mr. Joe, you have a lot of text messages from Emily."

I laughed out loud and said, "One day you'll understand…" and then, looking at her mom, I added, "You know when you know, right, Mom?"

She smiled, and I walked away toward the exit.

As I was walking toward the Delta parking lot I saw a man dressed in his full ACU outfit—a strong-looking fellow, about six foot three, two hundred and fifteen pounds. On his shoulder it said Army Ranger. I looked at him closely. His facial structure was very similar to someone I had just been talking to for the past three hours or so. Was it just a coincidence, or was there a family resemblance? Mary hadn't really told me much about her father. Just then, Mary and her mom came into sight and approached the man, eager and beaming. They embraced. It was her dad; he had returned from overseas safely!

After watching them greet each other for a couple seconds I turned away. As I turned my head I noticed the Army Ranger's right hand. He too wore the ring.

"Joe, Come on!"

My mom was right behind me in her car waiting for me to put my luggage in the trunk

"He too wears the ring," I whispered, then looked up to the sky and smiled. God meant for me to meet that little girl; our paths were meant to cross. I wonder if I'll ever see her or her father again. I guess only time will tell.

TO BE CONTINUED...

THE TRIP

As I wander in Life's forest
I am surrounded by great fears
This journey seems so long and hard,
I'm beset by falling tears.
From here the way seems hopeless
Cliffs and thorns align the way
The darkness that enfolds me
Makes me stumble and I stray.
The way is rough and rocky
Seems no light that can be found
Bruised and battered I give up,
A sobbing child upon the ground.
In my despair I hear a voice
It's small and still and quiet
It says, " My child just hold my hand
And things will be alright."
I recognize this still small voice
It's tried to speak before
But if I feel that I'm in charge,
When it speaks I close the door.
"Can I be sure you know the way
And you won't let me slip?
"Not only will I walk with you
IT WAS I WHO PLANNED THE TRIP."

EMILY GAY POE

Heading into the 2015 season, the jury was still out on new Citadel coach Mike Houston. The 42-year-old had great success at Division II Lenoir-Rhyne and came into his first Division I job at The Citadel saying that he expected to "compete for championships," and that his team would play with passion, physicality, and intensity.

But the results were not immediate. The Citadel opened the Mike Houston era with a 31-16 loss to Coastal Carolina, and in fact lost its first three games, four of its first five and six of its first eight under Houston, finishing his first season with a 5-7 overall record and 3-4 mark in the SoCon.

"Never again," vowed Houston after his first (and still only) losing season as a head coach. But the Bulldogs were picked to finish seventh in the SoCon in 2015, and after four games were sitting at 2-2 with their season hanging in the balance.

The turning point came in that fifth game, an October 10 contest with Wofford, which had beaten The Citadel an unfathomable 16 times in a row. Before a crowd of more than 10,000 at Johnson Hagood Memorial Stadium, sophomore quarterback Dominique Allen scored two touchdowns, and the Bulldogs' defense held the mighty Wofford rushing attack to 124 yards and 2.4 yards per carry in a 39-12 victory.

That was the first of five straight wins for the Bulldogs. But a 31-23 loss to No. 8 Chattanooga left The Citadel on the FCS playoff bubble at 7-3 overall and 6-1 in the SoCon heading into a Nov. 21 game at South Carolina. The Bulldogs had clinched a share of the SoCon title, but Chattanooga had earned the league's automatic bid to the playoffs. A loss to USC could conceivably leave The Citadel out of the playoffs.

Shockingly, the Bulldogs prevailed. Before a stunned crowd of 77,000 fans at Williams-Brice Stadium, Cam Jackson got the Bulldogs off to a quick start with a 59-yard TD run, and Tyler Renew finished off the Gamecocks with a 56-yard TD run in the fourth quarter. The defense held the Gamecocks to 72 rushing yards, and The Citadel's 23-22 win locked up a playoff bid and marked the second time since 1990 the Bulldogs had gone into Williams-Brice Stadium and won.

The momentum carried over into a wild 41-38, overtime win at Coastal Carolina to open the playoffs before the Bulldogs' dream season came to an end in a 14-6 loss at rival Charleston Southern. The Bulldogs had won as many as nine games for just the second time in school history and claimed the third SoCon championship in school history dating back to 1905. Houston would leave The Citadel after that season for James Madison, but the 2015 team had laid the foundation for a 2016 squad that went 10-2 and repeated as SoCon champs under coach Brent Thompson.

It's no stretch to say that the 2015 Bulldogs changed the game for modern Citadel football, showing that the military school could indeed compete for championships at the FCS level. A triple-option offense led by experienced linemen such as Sam Frye, Kyle Weaver and Ryan Bednar combined with a mature sophomore quarterback in Dominique Allen, talented slotback Cam Jackson and determined fullback Tyler Renew led the SoCon in rushing offense, total offense and total touchdowns. A defense stocked with playmaking linemen such as the late Mitchell Jeter and Joe Crochet, linebackers James Riley and Tevin Floyd and ball-hawking cornerback Dee Delaney, was second in the SoCon in scoring defense and total defense. Senior slotback Vinny Miller explained the turnaround of 2015.

„It was just a higher level of energy," said Miller. "I feel like there were higher expectations for us as far as our level of play goes. The coaches expect more from us and push us to a higher level. It was not hard to buy in with these guys, because you could see the level of passion in everything they do. That helps drive everything that we do."

Jeff Hartsell
Sports Reporter, *The Post and Courier*

23-22 12:00 PM ET November 21, 2015

Every year before the season started I knew whether or not that team was going to be good. This is the kind of stuff I guess players don't know about, but coaches sure do. I told Coach Houston we were going to be damn good that year. I don't know if you guys knew it or not, but he had called the defense that first year, and as we were going into the second year I begged him to let me call the defense. I wanted more say-so with Blake, the inside linebackers' coach; Tripp, the outside linebackers' coach; Joel, the safeties' coach; and Roy, the defensive line coach. We could all do it together, I said.

"Well, if we don't win, that's going to be your ass... It's your ass on the line," he said. But I wasn't worried. I believed in that team. The main reason for that is because of you guys. Y'all bought in and just gelled and glued and came together like I hadn't seen before in other teams that I have been a part of that have won championships. I remember telling him we were going to beat South Carolina. I told him that in the summer. One

thing that really stood out was that you guys were unselfish. You all were just selfless and it got to the point defensively where I knew with y'all it did not matter who made the play. A play didn't care who made it, and neither did you guys. It was a selfless attitude amongst that defense.

The proudest I was of you guys was when we lost in that Charleston Southern game round two of the FCS playoffs. I mean we kicked their tail up and down that field. If I am not mistaken, our offense had five turnovers that game, three of which were on our side of the field inside the 20-yard line, and we only lost by less than a score. You guys played your tails off. I mean I was so proud of you guys. I did not want it to end, because I knew we had more in our tank. I knew we could go further, but I am just so proud of you guys.

You all had your heads held high and you finished. You know, coming in with a new coaching staff regime, you guys could have squawked at it, you could have been these guys don't know what they are talking about, but all of you bought in. You guys bought in....

I am just so thankful for you guys giving me the opportunity to allow me to be the defensive coordinator and to be a voice. To this day I talk to some of the guys and we say our motto, "We all we got," and they respond, "We all we need." I mean, I felt like that culture that was built between us allowed us to be successful. I just wish we could have done a little more because that team, The Citadel 2015 Bulldogs, was special!

Coach Maurice Drayton
NFL Coach for the Green Bay Packers
& 2015 Defensive Coordinator at The Citadel

Shoot, man, that 2015 team wasn't just one of the best teams I've ever been on or in the country. It was the most positive energy I've ever been around, man. Everyone that played on that team had the same mission, obviously, which was to win games; but I think our connection off the field *and in the locker room was the driving force behind why we were so successful. We invested more into each other than anything else.*

On the field, shoot, that spoke for itself. That defense was relentless. Knocking fools out, picking the ball off, scoring... everything you could've wanted from a defense could've been found in us! When I was with the Arizona Cardinals I had people coming up to me telling me how good we were and how they knew we were going to beat the University of South Carolina and everything. From the front 5, to the LB's, and the DB's... that was the most complete unit in the country! I've never felt anything like what I felt on that team. The hardest-working individuals I've ever known were on that team. But like I said, the football aspect of that team spoke for itself. The investment we made in each other's life off the field was the fuel for our successes. True love!

Tevin Floyd
Former NFL Arizona Cardinals Linebacker
& All-Conference Linebacker at The Citadel

The 2015 season will go down as my favorite and most fun football season of my entire career. After two years of tough seasons and close losses, we knew as rising upperclassmen of that team that there was a change needed to happen to achieve what the coaches were asking of us. All the way from winter workouts, spring ball, and summer workouts we meshed together and held each other accountable. No one slacked off, and I swear our practices were harder than the actual games. We prided ourselves in working harder than everyone and punishing each and every team every weekend. That team was a brotherhood, and that's why I believe we were so successful. Brothers who held each other accountable.

Tyler Renew
Former NFL Atlanta Falcon's Running Back
& All-American B-Back at The Citadel

I think the 2015 was the best team in school history because it was the start of a back-to- back championship. We all just bonded together as one and trusted one another.

Dee Delaney
NFL Defensive Back for the Jacksonville Jaguars
& Former All-American DB at The Citadel

I think a large part of our success came from our senior leadership and believing that we could accomplish our goal. We set a goal to win the conference in the off season and everyone bought in and trusted the process that would take us to get there. That huge leap of faith allowed us to have the confidence we needed to make those big plays in crunch time moments when we needed them!

Dominique Allen
Former Quarterback at The Citadel

It all turned around when the school hired Coach Houston and his staff. They breathed life into the program. They changed the culture quickly and we all bought in. After that we just put in the work and followed the plan. Playing football became fun again and when the guys started having fun, winning came naturally.

Alex Glover
Former Wide Receiver and Tight End at The Citadel

We as a group made it our goal to have as much fun as we could my senior year. We won a lot and had a lot of fun. I credit much of our success to the brotherhood we had as a team led by the class of 2016.

Eric Goins,
Former All-Conference Kicker and Punter at The Citadel

The 2015 team was the most fun, talented, and closest group of guys that I ever played with at The Citadel, and it showed in our performance!

Kyle Weaver, MBA
Former All-Conference Offensive Guard at The Citadel

What made that team different was we truly bought in and trusted in the process, especially in the offseason, and on game day we believed in each other no matter who we played.

Caleb Bennett,
Former Linebacker at The Citadel

Our players spend a lot of time outside of their comfort zone. There's no naptime in the middle of the day. When I was in school if I had a break between classes, I'd go back to my room and chill out. These guys don't have that. The academics here are extremely challenging. There's a whole element of leadership training that goes on top of their coursework and it doesn't matter if you're an engineer, an exercise science major, or a business major — you have more classes on top of your course load than you do at a normal college. We want to play a team in the worst conditions possible, because we can function in the worst conditions possible.

Donnell Boucher
Head Strength and Conditioning Coach at The Citadel

CPSIA information can be obtained
at www.ICGtesting.com
Printed in the USA
LVHW030903031218
599057LV00007B/326

9 781977 204554